Excerpts from unsolicited letter
In Christ Ministries from peopl
this series:

*I can truly say that, after finding
the fullness of my spiritual freed
nificant moment of my life.*

*The release that I felt as years of shame and bondage were lifted from
me is hard to describe. I really do not know what to say – I feel like a
human being again!*

*My life has been transformed. It truly was like walking from darkness
back into light again.*

*FICM provided the tool which has allowed me to break the sin-repent-
cycle. I am full of hope for the future.*

I am a new person and everyone has seen the difference.

*Even though I work for a church and have done many things for God,
my walk had become a laboured trudge. Yet now I feel so at peace.*

I have a clear head, praise Jesus – it hadn't been clear for years!

Finding my freedom in Christ has changed my life.

*The everyday problems of life that once seemed so insurmountable
are now well in perspective and I am able to tackle most of them in a
calm and rational way.*

*It has transformed my life. I now know God always loves me even
though sometimes I might stray from the path he has mapped out for
me. I know God is always there, and I marvel at the truth about his
kindness, his generosity, and his feelings towards me.*

*When my ex-husband left, I felt like half a person. I didn't think I
should be alone and I didn't feel whole. Those feelings have gone. I feel
fulfilled in who I am and am happy with my life.*

FREEDOM **IN**CHRIST *Discipleship Series* **BOOK 3**

BREAK FREE, STAY FREE

DON'T LET THE PAST HOLD YOU BACK

STEVE GOSS

MONARCH
B O O K S
Oxford, UK & Grand Rapids, Michigan, USA

Published by Monarch Books
an imprint of
Lion Hudson plc
Wilkinson House, Jordan Hill Road,
Oxford OX2 8DR, England
monarch@lionhudson.com
www.lionhudson.com/monarch

ISBN: 978-1-85424-859-6

Printed and bound in Great Britain by
Marston Book Services Ltd, Oxfordshire

First edition 2008

Acknowledgments
Unless otherwise stated, Scripture quotations are taken from the Holy
Bible, New International Version, © 1973, 1978, 1984 by the International
Bible Society. Used by permission of Hodder and Stoughton Ltd. All rights
reserved.

A catalogue record for this book is available from the British Library.

*This book is dedicated to Sophie,
a wonderful young lady who hears God's voice and responds.
We love spending time together. I am so grateful to her
for the generous way she has released me,
especially at weekends,
to minister away from home.*

Contents

A Special Word of Thanks

I have learned just about everything I know about helping people become fruitful disciples from Neil Anderson, author of *The Bondage Breaker*, *Victory Over the Darkness* and many other books. These are now regarded by many Christians as classics, and rightly so.

It has been my immense privilege to spend time with Neil, to sit under his teaching at many conferences, to collaborate with him in writing *The Freedom In Christ Discipleship Course*, and to have the opportunity to put my questions to him while we were 'on the road' together.

One of the first things I did when I sensed that the Lord might be prompting me to write this series, was to ask Neil if he minded. After all, the way he has taught these great biblical principles of freedom is so much part of me now, that I could not possibly write these books without using his fundamental methodology.

He had every right to say no and if he had done that I would have dropped the project there and then. However, he positively encouraged me to get started.

For that, and for all he has taught to so many over the years, I am indebted to this man of God who continues to travel the world with this life-changing message.

My thanks go too to Tony Collins and Rod Shepherd at Monarch for their help in getting this series off the ground, as well as to the fantastic team at Freedom In Christ Ministries for their constant support and sacrificial service in taking this message to churches around the country.

Foreword

For twenty-five years I believed in God and regularly attended church. If anyone asked me about my beliefs, I told them that I was a Christian. I looked like a Christian and generally acted like one. In Europe and North America if one respected their parents and wanted to be a 'good boy or girl' it was the cultural thing to be and do. It is sobering to look back and realize that I was one of those millions of cultural 'Christians' who don't have an authentic relationship with their Creator and Heavenly Father. If God hadn't intervened in my life I would have become like the rest of those disillusioned by religion and joined the pagan parade now exiting the culturally or politically correct 'church'.

Religion is the curse of this world, and the force behind many of the conflicts plaguing the planet. However, a relationship with God is our only hope. I was the senior warden of an Episcopal (Anglican) Church and working as an aerospace engineer when I was invited to attend a lay institute for evangelism. I didn't know what that was and had I known I probably wouldn't have gone. The priest wanted me to go with him. So I did, and while learning to share my faith I realized I didn't have any. The presenter asked what difference it would make in our religious beliefs if Christ hadn't come in the flesh? I didn't have an answer. I believed in God and that was enough. Wasn't it?

I heard the gospel for the first time, and gladly gave my heart to Christ and was born again. I became a new creation in Christ, but it took me several years to fully understand what that really meant. At first I was really excited about my new-found faith, and at the same time disappointed in myself for playing 'church' all those years. I couldn't help but wonder how many others were going through the same motions and missing the real relationship that God wants us to have with himself.

Two years later I sensed the call of God to go into full time ministry. The past forty years have been an exciting adventure of learning, growing, and discovering how God sets captives free and binds up their broken hearts. My dear friends and colleagues, Steve and Zoë Goss, have been going through the same transformation and now God is using them to accomplish his work in the United Kingdom.

In writing these four discipleship books, Steve has done a masterful work in presenting the core message of Freedom In Christ Ministries. You will learn, as we have, what difference Christ makes in our 'religious beliefs'. Jesus is the One who died for the sin that has separated us from God. Jesus rose from the dead in order that we can have new life in him. His sacrificial life, death and resurrection also disarmed the god of this world (Colossians 2:15). Jesus came to undo the works of Satan (1 John 3:8) who has deceived the world (Revelation 12:9), and has it under his control (1 John 5:19).

The Church is not an institution for religious observances. It is not an organization, it is an organism. The Church is the body of Christ. The membership is made up of born-again believers who are alive and free in Christ. Their names are written in the Lamb's book of life. 'As many as received him, to them he gave the right to become children of God, to those who believe in his name' (John 1:12). You will discover this and much more as you work your way through this series of discipleship books. So welcome to the family of God. You have many spiritual brothers and sisters in Christ who are learning and growing just as you are. "The Holy Spirit is bearing witness with your spirit that you are a child of God" (Romans 8:16). Have you ever considered what an incredible privilege it is to be called a child of God? The grace of God is truly amazing, and may you grow in that grace and become all that your Heavenly Father created you to be.

Dr. Neil T. Anderson
Founder and President Emeritus of Freedom In Christ Ministries

PART 1

Four Key Principles

We drove home from Judy's house on the motorway, about a 35-minute journey, in our ageing Peugeot 205 GTi. I loved driving that car. It was small but very fast. And noisy. It was the noise that prevented us from hearing my mobile phone ringing repeatedly from my coat on the back seat. It wasn't until we got back home and switched the ignition off that we heard it. This time, however, it was not Judy, who had repeatedly been trying to get us since we had left her. It was Terry, our pastor. He told us that Judy had just called him to say she had taken an overdose. He knew we had been seeing her and wondered where we were.

In fact, we had spent a couple of hours with Judy that morning because we knew she was in a hard place. A Christian who had approached our church for help, she was struggling with a lot of nasty things that had been done to her as a child. We (my wife and I, that is) had gone over simply to spend some time with her and encourage her. We had left her in reasonable shape, or so we thought. But as soon as we left, she downed a load of prescription drugs and called us. I guess she didn't want us to leave, and this was a cry for help from someone who was desperate and didn't know what else to do. She thought we would get the call and come straight back – but we didn't hear the phone.

I called Judy and was relieved when she answered the

phone. I ascertained what she had taken and phoned the emergency services, who said she needed treatment and sent an ambulance immediately. We caught up with her a little later at the hospital casualty department.

That was a low point for Judy and also for us in our dealings with her. It brought home to me just how desperate you can become if you are unable to resolve painful issues from the past.

Today Judy seems like a completely different person. She is one of the most fruitful Christians I know. She is free from the stuff that for decades had dragged her down. Only yesterday I took a call from someone who told me just what an inspiration Judy has been to her.

My upbringing was quite different from Judy's. My parents have always been loving, caring and kind, and protected me from trauma from events outside the family. I do not have anything like the same issues from the past to deal with as she had.

But I now realize that for years I too was held back by stuff from the past. It kept me going round in circles as a Christian and was preventing me from becoming all that God wanted me to be. In my case it didn't show up in dramatic episodes such as suicide attempts. It was much less obvious. It would be a sense that, despite the fact that I professed to believe that money does not make you happy, I persisted in spending most of my efforts in life on building a career that I hoped (secretly at least!) would bring me lots of money. It showed in my conviction that, although I admired Christians who 'stepped out in faith', ultimately I would always play it safe. It showed in getting caught in what I would now call 'sin–confess cycles', where I would just keep returning to the same old sin time after time and could not seem to escape. It could also be seen in the kind of relationship I had with God – formal more than friendly. I did what I perceived to be 'the right things', so I appeared to be 'a good Christian', I'm sure. But looking back, I am amazed at how much stuff I was carrying around.

I have yet to meet a Christian who did not have 'stuff' from the past that could usefully be resolved in order for them to become more fruitful. Whether your 'stuff' is more akin to Judy's or more like mine, this book will show why you can expect to walk completely free from it and how to get started.

In the first part of this book we will look at four key principles. Then in the second part we'll examine how practically we can dismantle the effects of the past so that we can go on to become the people God wants us to be.

Principle 1

Don't Just Cope with the Past – Resolve It!

Think for a moment about some Christians you know, perhaps people in your church. Can you picture them? Who do you think are the ones whom God is most likely to use to do great things? What are their characteristics?

Just occasionally you can read something in the Bible and it hits you like a brick between the eyes. I had one of those moments as I was reading Isaiah 61. This is the passage that Jesus read out in the synagogue on an occasion when he was back in Nazareth, his home town. It caused quite a commotion. When he had finished, he turned and said to the people who were there, 'Today this scripture is fulfilled in your hearing' (Luke 4:21). This led eventually to them taking him out and threatening to throw him off a cliff. This is what it says:

The Spirit of the Sovereign Lord is on me, because the Lord has anointed me to preach good news to the poor. He has sent me to bind up the broken-hearted, to proclaim freedom for the captives and release from darkness for the prisoners, to proclaim the year of the Lord's favour and the day of vengeance of our God, to comfort all who mourn, and provide for those who grieve in Zion – to bestow on them a crown of beauty instead of ashes, the oil of gladness instead of mourning, and a garment of praise instead of a spirit of despair.

Jesus was saying that he was the fulfilment of this passage. In a real sense, he used it as the 'manifesto' for his ministry. What does it tell us about him?

First and foremost, what comes across is that the people that he is particularly concerned to help are those in desperate situations: the poor (the Hebrew word literally means 'pressed down' or 'depressed', either in mind or circumstances, not just financially poor); the broken-hearted; those held in captivity; those in darkness. He came to bring to them the exact opposite of what they are currently experiencing: captives are set free; those who mourn find comfort; those who are in despair see that despair turn to praise.

I have always known that Jesus has a heart for those in trouble and that he came to negate that trouble. However, it's the next few verses that hit me between the eyes, because they go further – much further:

> *They will be called oaks of righteousness, a planting of the Lord for the display of his splendour. They will rebuild the ancient ruins and restore the places long devastated; they will renew the ruined cities that have been devastated for generations.*

These weak, vulnerable people, the ones whom society writes off, are the ones who will be called 'oaks of righteousness'. They are the ones who will rebuild and bring restoration. Which of your Christian friends did you picture as the ones through whom God is most likely to do great things? His heart, of course, is to do them through every Christian. But his special delight is to see it happen through those who are poor, weak, vulnerable and apparently hopeless.

The whole point of Jesus' ministry was to see those who are downtrodden, those in bondage, those who think there is no possibility whatsoever that they could be the ones God uses, completely turned around. These are the people who read the inspirational Christian books and listen to the messages.

They believe that God will work through others. But not in their wildest dreams could he ever use them. Read the passage again! That is the glorious heart of God: to enable those with no hope or obvious resources to be the ones who bring blessing, restoration and hope. He did not come simply to help them *cope* with their difficult circumstances. He came to bring about a complete transformation.

There is a huge consequence here, one that has been largely lost in many parts of the church. It is this: Christians do not simply have to learn to live with the negative effects of their past – they can fully expect to resolve them completely.

How did Jesus' ministry accomplish that? Let's consider two reasons we are given for his coming. Firstly, Jesus said, 'I have come that they may have life, and have it to the full' (John 10:10). Before he came, we were all destined to live with the consequences of Adam's sin. Created to be spiritually alive, to be secure, significant and accepted, Adam threw that spiritual life away when he was deceived by Satan and gave in to temptation. As a result, all his descendants were born physically alive but spiritually dead, desperate for the security, significance and acceptance they were created for, desperate for an intimate relationship with God, but instead being simply 'objects of wrath' (Ephesians 2:3). Jesus came to change all that. We deserved nothing but hell. He took the punishment we deserved in his own body. He satisfied the righteous anger of God. With that out of the way, we could be spiritually reconnected to God. That made us completely new – 'new creations', as Paul put it (2 Corinthians 5:17). Although our physical bodies did not change, inside we are totally different. We have been restored to the life we were always meant to have, the life that Adam and Eve had before the Fall.

When we still had our old nature, we had little hope of resolving past issues. It's a whole different ballgame when you are a holy child of the Living God.

Secondly, 'The reason the Son of God appeared was to

destroy the devil's work' (1 John 3:8). He did not come to put a plaster over the devil's work. He came to destroy it. When I see a Christian carrying a lot of damage from the past, I know that God's heart is to see all of that damage done away with and that Christian living in their new identity. And I know it's a distinct possibility. In fact, it should be the norm. Satan cannot stop it happening, because in Christ we have much more power and authority than he will ever have. We are seated with Christ at the right hand of God, the ultimate seat of power and authority. At the cross Jesus completely disarmed Satan (Colossians 2:15).

It is on that basis – the fact that we are 'new creations' seated with Christ and have real spiritual life – that we can say with confidence that the negative effects of the past can be completely resolved in Christ.

A Christian can expect to resolve issues that a not-yet-Christian has no choice but to try to live with. It's all down to the astonishing truth of what happened to you the moment you became a Christian. This is covered in detail in the first book in this series. In short, whereas at one time we were fundamentally, by our very nature, displeasing to God, we have been changed inside into people who actually share God's nature. We are holy and righteous. We need no longer define ourselves as 'sinners' but as 'saints'.

Let me contrast that for a moment with someone who is not yet a Christian. I see no basis for them to resolve those negative effects. Sure, they can expect to make progress with good support and advice, but I don't hold out much hope for them to resolve completely the effects of the past. That is borne out by secular counselling, where the goal by and large is to give people strategies to cope with the effects of the past, to help them live with those negative effects. That is commendable. However, in the case of a Christian, a new creation, we can expect much more. Jesus did not come to change the past.

But he did come to enable Christians to walk completely free of those negative effects.

That is why, when someone tells me they are going to see a Christian counsellor, I always advise them to ask whether that counsellor has what might be called 'a theology of resolution' or is in fact, at heart, using secular methods whose objective is simply to help them cope. The outcome is likely to be hugely different.

At one of our conferences, we were richly blessed by a wonderful guy from Glasgow who turned up with some songs he had written, reflecting his own journey to freedom from a life of addiction and abuse. Talking of his experience with a counsellor using methods designed simply to help him cope, he said to me, 'It was as if I was carrying around a can of worms. I'd go to my counsellor and we'd get the tin out, take off the lid, take out one or two of the worms, poke them a bit and talk about them. Then I'd have to put them back in the tin and carry them around again. Except, every time I put them back in, it was harder and harder to put the lid on. Now I've opened the tin and thrown the worms away. In fact, I've thrown the tin away too!'

I met a lovely lady called Cheryl who had been dealt a bad hand in life. As a result of bad experiences in her childhood, she became a prostitute and a drug addict and for many years she lived that lifestyle, until one day she was at a very low point and, as she describes it, Jesus appeared to her in her bedroom and said he wanted to heal her. She thought she had better find a church. She went to a large church and did her best to fit in, but every week she found herself in tears, unable to function. She went forward time after time for prayer but nothing changed. The church tired of her and she concluded that she just couldn't do it. She stopped going along and fell back into her old lifestyle.

Thankfully, the story does not end there. She found her way to another church that knew how to help her dump the rubbish from the past and become a fruitful disciple. Today she is one of the most fruitful Christians in that church. She has gone from being one church's basket-case to another church's star discipler because she came across people who understood how to apply practically what Isaiah 61 is talking about.

There are many people like Cheryl in our churches who are carrying a lot of what might be called 'baggage'. There are a lot of things that they need to resolve. The truth is that is not particularly difficult now that they are new creations, but if they join a church that is unable to help them deal with the footholds of the enemy in their lives or explain to them how to take hold of their freedom in Christ and stand firm, what is the likely outcome? They will probably make a genuine attempt to do their best at 'being a Christian' but will become increasingly troubled by the negative thoughts in their minds or the patterns of sin they don't seem to be able to break, and will eventually give up. To my mind that is one of the main reasons that we see many new Christians simply falling away after a few weeks or months.

A lot of people in our churches are doing their best to 'act like Christians' in the hope that they will become 'like everyone else'. They end up either living a kind of double life or walking away. I too spent years trying to behave as I thought a Christian should behave, all the while struggling. The irony, of course, is that the answer comes when they realize that they don't have to 'act' like a Christian, they simply have to be themselves: pure, holy, new creations who have the power and authority to kick the enemy out of their lives and grow.

In this book, we will examine how practically we can stop the past holding us back. No one can change the past but by God's grace, every Christian can walk free of it.

Are you simply a result of your past experiences, of your past history? No, not any more. Now you are a result of what Christ did on the cross. You are a new creation.

Principle 2

Take the Whole of Reality into Account

The fact that we are new creations and can therefore expect to walk free from the effects of the past is no guarantee that we actually will.

> *To the Jews who had believed him, Jesus said, 'If you hold to my teaching, you are really my disciples. Then you will know the truth, and the truth will set you free.'* (JOHN 8:31–32)

Freedom comes when we know the truth. If someone does not know the truth, how do you enlighten them? With our Western worldview, we assume that all we have to do is tell them. And if they don't get it the first time, tell them again…and again…

However, that is to ignore the reality of the battle that we are in. Jesus told a story that illustrates perfectly why just being told the truth does not mean that we know the truth. It was a story about a man who went out to sow seed. The seed prospered according to where it fell:

> *Some fell along the path; it was trampled on, and the birds of the air ate it up. Some fell on rock, and when it came up, the plants withered because they had no moisture. Other seed fell among thorns, which grew up with it and choked the plants. Still other seed fell on good soil. It came up and yielded a crop, a hundred times more than was sown.* (LUKE 8:5–8)

He went on to explain his illustration as follows:

> *The seed is the word of God. Those along the path are the ones who hear, and then the devil comes and takes away the word from their hearts, so that they may not believe and be saved. Those on the rock are the ones who receive the word with joy when they hear it, but they have no root. They believe for a while, but in the time of testing they fall away. The seed that fell among thorns stands for those who hear, but as they go on their way they are choked by life's worries, riches and pleasures, and they do not mature. But the seed on good soil stands for those with a noble and good heart, who hear the word, retain it, and by persevering produce a crop.*
>
> (LUKE 8:11–15)

God is the God of all truth. When he says something, it is by definition true. When God says how reality is, that really is how it is. On the face of it, you would not think that knowing the truth would be that difficult. However, when God's Word of truth comes to us through a Bible study, listening to a talk in church, reading a Christian book or whatever other method he uses, it would be a mistake to assume that we are operating in an environment that includes just us and God.

Whether we like it or not, we are in the middle of a pitched battle with others involved. It's a battle for truth that takes place in our minds. Since our first breath we have been conditioned to challenge how God says reality is by our three enemies, the world, the flesh and the devil.

Like a bird stealing seeds before they are able to take root, the devil is constantly trying to take God's Word away from us. He is out to 'steal and kill and destroy' (John 10:10). His incessant question to us, usually spoken through the world and the flesh, is the same one he posed to Eve in the garden and to Jesus when he was being tempted in the wilderness: 'Did God *really* say....?' If he is given influence through unresolved sin,

Satan is able to blind us to the truth. We can try and try to take hold of truth but we will not be able to.

The 'flesh' refers to habits of thinking that we have got into over the years, especially as we tried to meet our legitimate needs for security, significance and acceptance without God. These thought patterns become our 'default' behaviours and remain so unless we take positive action to change them. The flesh comes at us from inside, forever trying to pull us back to old thought patterns based on lies ('I'm useless', 'I'm dirty', 'I'm not like other Christians – this may work for them but it won't work for me'). It also tries to persuade us that it can meet our legitimate needs for security, significance and acceptance through money, sex, food, drugs or, in fact, anything other than 'the God of all comfort' (2 Corinthians 1:3). If we allow it to dominate, it becomes difficult for the seed of God's Word to prosper and we are likely to fall away when things get tough.

The world system in which we grew up tries to impose its own view of reality on us. That 'worldview' varies according to where and when we were brought up. It comes at us from outside and constantly tests us by directly challenging how God says it is. We have been conditioned to see God as removed and impersonal. In reality he actually lives within us and takes an interest in every detail of our lives. We have been conditioned to see ourselves as insignificant. The truth is that, if you had been the only person in the world throughout history who needed to be saved, Jesus would have died just for you – you are that special. In the West we have been conditioned to assume that reality is just what we can detect with our senses. It is far more than that – the unseen world is just as real as the world we can see.

The world also throws worries at us and tempts us with pleasure. When we get wrapped up in those things instead of seeking God's Kingdom first, our spiritual growth is stunted and we do not mature.

The Christians who bear fruit and mature are those who hear the Word, retain it and persevere. But how do you do that? What makes the difference between a person who hears but has the Word snatched away and one who hears and retains?

Look back at the verses we quoted at the beginning of this section. Jesus said that knowing the truth starts when we hold to his teaching. In other words, we initiate the process that leads eventually to the truth setting us free by making a conscious decision to hold to his teaching.

What does 'holding to his teaching' mean? Many see Jesus as a moral teacher who came to give us a set of rules – his 'teaching' – to live by. Actually, he did no such thing. God had already done that by giving us 'the Law' hundreds of years before Christ came. It hadn't worked. Paul tells us that the whole point of the rules that made up the Law was to show us that with our old fallen human nature we simply could not keep them. That, in turn, was specifically intended to make us aware of our need for Christ (Galatians 3:24–25).

Jesus came so that the concept of trying to justify our-selves through keeping a set of rules could be replaced by the concept of being justified through faith in Christ and then going on to walk by faith. In practice, walking by faith in Christ boils down to seeing the world as God sees it (that is, as it really is) and acting accordingly. We are saved when we understand that we cannot save ourselves and accept Christ's free gift of life. We hold to Jesus' teaching when we fall in line with how he says the world is and act accordingly. If we ignore part of that reality – for example, the fact that we operate in an unseen spiritual world as well as in the material world that we can see – we will struggle. The Western worldview predisposes us to do just that, and we need perseverance and determina-tion to 'hold' to Jesus' teaching.

We looked in detail in the second book in this series at the nature of the battle we are in and how to ensure that we win it. Suffice to say here that if we do not take all of reality into account, we will tend to live as though the spiritual world is not real. It can make a huge difference. My favourite example of this in the Bible is the servant of Elisha:

> When the servant of the man of God got up and went out early the next morning, an army with horses and chariots had surrounded the city. 'Oh, my lord, what shall we do?' the servant asked. 'Don't be afraid,' the prophet answered. 'Those who are with us are more than those who are with them.' And Elisha prayed, 'O Lord, open his eyes so he may see.' Then the Lord opened the servant's eyes, and he looked and saw the hills full of horses and chariots of fire all around Elisha.
>
> (2 KINGS 6:15–17)

All he could see was two of them against a whole army. He needed to see the whole of reality, with an unseen world that is just as real as the world we can see. We too need to remind ourselves constantly of this fact. Paul prayed this for the Ephesian church:

> I pray also that the eyes of your heart may be enlightened in order that you may know the hope to which he has called you, the riches of his glorious inheritance in the saints, and his incomparably great power for us who believe. That power is like the working of his mighty strength, which he exerted in Christ when he raised him from the dead and seated him at his right hand in the heavenly realms, far above all rule and authority, power and dominion, and every title that can be given, not only in the present age but also in the one to come. And God placed all things under his feet and appointed him to be head over everything for the church, which is his body, the fullness of him who fills everything in every way.
>
> (EPHESIANS 1:18–23)

There is a very large gap between the messages that constantly come at us day in, day out from the world, the flesh and the devil, and the way things actually are. We too need 'the eyes of our heart' to be enlightened. It's all too easy to think, for example, that we are lacking something. Maybe we think we lack power and are asking God for more. However, nowhere in the Bible are Christians instructed to ask God for more power. Why not? Look at that passage again and see just how much we already have! Does it *feel* like it? Probably not. But that's not the point.

Christians who grow to maturity are the ones who are prepared time and again to come back to what God says is true and act on that basis rather than being led by their feelings or circumstances. The more they do this, the more they realize that it actually works, that how God says things are, really is true. That makes it easier (but not necessarily easy!) next time.

Principle 3

Know Who is Responsible for What

Having faith is just seeing things as they really are and acting accordingly. Part of taking the whole of reality into account is realizing that God has set the world up in a certain way, and he has decreed that some things are his responsibility and some things are my responsibility. God will not do for me the things that he has said are for me to do.

Unfortunately, we tend to get this the wrong way round. We want to do the things that are his responsibility and we want him to do the things that are our responsibility. Let me illustrate.

Whose responsibility is it to ensure that you have enough money? Whatever your answer to that question, an impartial observer looking at the way we live might well conclude that we believe that it is our responsibility. Biblically, it is not. The biblical principle is this:

> *So do not worry, saying, 'What shall we eat?' or 'What shall we drink?' or 'What shall we wear?' For the pagans run after all these things, and your heavenly Father knows that you need them. But seek first his kingdom and his righteousness, and all these things will be given to you as well.* (MATTHEW 6:31–33)

Our responsibility is to seek God's Kingdom and his right-eousness – in other words, to do what is right. Then we can expect God to do the part that is his responsibility – to provide everything we need so that we don't have to busy ourselves with that.

Paul commends the Philippian Christians for abiding by this principle. He praises them for sending financial gifts and says, 'They are a fragrant offering, an acceptable sacrifice, pleasing to God. And my God will meet all your needs according to his glorious riches in Christ Jesus' (Philippians 4:18b–19).

Often just the last sentence of this passage is quoted, as if God will always meet all our needs, regardless of our actions. In fact, that promise is made in the context of our first fulfilling our responsibility – in this case, giving.

So we have a responsibility to live righteously, which includes working, if we are able (see Ephesians 4:28), and giving away a portion of what the Lord gives us. Once we have done that, we can sit back because it is God's responsibility to meet our needs – and, of course, he will.

Let's try another example. Whose responsibility is it to make things happen in the area of service that God has given you? If, for example, you are in some kind of leadership role in your church, whose responsibility is it to ensure that the church grows and flourishes? Here is the biblical principle: 'Unless the Lord builds the house, its builders labour in vain' (Psalm 127:1).

If you are a leader of a ministry or working in your own personal ministry, it's difficult to let it go and let God build it. If we know what needs to be done, we are tempted simply to do it. However, if we do not let God build, in my experience God waits until we realize that we can't do it in our own strength and finally step back and let him in. Sometimes he has to wait a long time for us to come to the end of our own resources. In fact, our responsibility is to be still before him and wait patiently for him (Psalm 37:7), pray and then simply do what he tells us to do, leaving the outcome to him.

Nothing will interfere more in the process of growing to

maturity than us trying to get God to do in our lives what he has said is our responsibility, or trying to get someone else to do what is our responsibility. Conversely, we can hold someone back if we try to play God's role in their life.

In the second book in this series, I mentioned the young lady who approached me after a conference, saying that every night she was woken by a scary demonic presence in her room. She was in her mid twenties, had moved into a flat of her own but at that point had moved back in with her parents and actually got into bed with them each night when the scary manifestations occurred. She kept praying that God would take the scary presence away, but he never did, and it reduced her practically to a nervous wreck.

So why did God not take it away? Was he being cruel? Why did he not answer her heartfelt prayer repeated night after night? Actually, he had already answered it long before she prayed it. At the cross he completely disarmed Satan (Colossians 2:15) and gave us power and authority over him. It's a question of understanding who is responsible for what. In his wisdom, God had said that dealing with this issue was her responsibility: 'Submit to God. Resist the devil and he will flee from you' (James 4:7). Who was the one who had to do the submitting and resisting? She was!

When I explained to her that she had the power, authority and responsibility to do that, her first response was, 'I couldn't. I'm not strong enough.' However, she committed herself to God's Word rather than her feelings, and came bounding up to me the next day, saying, 'Guess what. It worked!' Walking by faith – that is to say, acting on how God says the world is – always works!

Most defeated Christians are in effect hoping that God will change his ways to accommodate them – 'Please God, bend the rules just this once, just for me.' They want God to assume their responsibility. He won't – for their own good. If he had stepped in to 'humour' this young lady and had done what was hers to do, she would never have learned the crucial lesson of just how much power and authority she has in Christ. Now that she has learned that lesson, she need never be troubled by the same issue again. She took a big step towards becoming a mature Christian. If God had stepped in and bent the rules, she would have learned nothing.

Where there is a problem

There's only one place in the Bible that gives any kind of detailed instructions on what to do if someone is in trouble or sick. It's James 5:13–16:

> *Is any one of you in trouble? He should pray. Is anyone happy? Let him sing songs of praise. Is any one of you sick? He should call the elders of the church to pray over him and anoint him with oil in the name of the Lord. And the prayer offered in faith will make the sick person well; the Lord will raise him up. If he has sinned, he will be forgiven. Therefore confess your sins to each other and pray for each other so that you may be healed. The prayer of a righteous man is powerful and effective.*

When we read this passage, it's all too easy to dwell on an obscure point. 'Hmm, I wonder what kind of oil I should use… Does it have to be extra-virgin olive oil or would a little of the oil for my car do the trick?' In fact, the great point behind this passage is understanding who is responsible for what in this kind of situation.

The struggling person needs to take the initiative

To start with, it's the struggling person who needs to take the initiative. The one who is in trouble is to pray. The one who is sick is to call the elders of the church.

I have a friend who is a pastor. He told me that a lady in his congregation who is usually friendly started giving him the cold shoulder. He asked her if anything was wrong. 'You didn't visit me when I was in hospital!' she said. 'What, you've been in hospital?' he replied. It was as if she expected him to have such a hotline to God that he would know she had a problem without being told. In fact, she had a responsibility to take the initiative, to let him know, at which point he would have been only too happy to visit her and do what God had given him the responsibility to do.

They need to confess and repent

Look again at this verse and note the order in which things are to be done:

> *Therefore confess your sins to each other and pray for each other so that you may be healed. The prayer of a righteous man is powerful and effective.*

If you prayed for someone and you later discovered that they were locked into sins of pride, bitterness and rebellion, would you be surprised if God did not answer your prayer? Of course not. 'If I had cherished sin in my heart, the Lord would not have listened' (Psalm 66:18). It's essential that they first take on board their responsibility to confess their sins.

Confession is simply agreeing with God – being honest. All secular counsellors will tell you that healing starts with honesty – facing up to the truth.

Repentance takes it further. It is actively shutting the door on the sin, taking back any ground given to the enemy and changing the way we think.

We will look later at how our sin gives the devil a 'foothold' which he uses to hold us back. Becoming a Christian does not automatically remove those footholds. We need specifically to renounce each one. Renouncing past activities that have opened the door to Satan's influence in our lives is a critical part of repentance – something, again, that is our responsibility alone. If we don't do it, we leave the enemy room to influence our thinking. There is a battle going on for our minds all the time.

They need to pray

I was part of the teaching team at a large Christian conference, and one evening in a gathering of several thousand people, participants were given the opportunity to respond to God and come forward for prayer. A large number came forward and queues formed in front of those of us who, as part of the team, were designated to pray with them. The first person in my queue was a young man in his early twenties. I asked him why he had come forward and he said, 'I'm at a crossroads in my career. I don't know whether to go and pursue one job or take a different direction.' I asked him what he was hoping I could do and he said, 'I'd like you to pray about it and tell me which direction to take.'

That seemed like a pretty tall order to me! The thought was going through my mind, 'Well, I'm happy to pray, but why would God tell me the answer to that prayer? Surely he would rather tell you…' I'm a father of two daughters and I have an equal relationship with them. However, it does occasionally happen that one of them thinks that if she asks for something, I'll be less likely to assent to it than if she gets her sister to ask on her behalf, 'Dad, my sister wants to go out to the cinema with her friends again tonight. Will you let her?' Of course, I simply say, 'Get her to ask me herself.'

In this case too, I asked the young man to pray to God himself. I could see exactly what was going on in his mind:

'Oh no, this happens to me in the supermarket – I always pick the wrong queue! This guy doesn't understand the rules. He's a "speaker" so obviously much more in touch with God than I am. He's supposed to pray and then tell me what God is saying.' In fact, he graciously humoured me and he prayed. What happened next was extraordinary. It turned out that God, at that time, was not particularly interested in which career option he chose. Instead God wanted him to know how special he was and that he did not have to strive any more in order to please him. I hardly said a thing. God spoke to him.

So why would someone want me to ask God something when they can ask him themselves? The answer, of course, is that they think I must somehow be more 'spiritual' or 'anointed' so am better able to hear God.

That kind of thing happens to me fairly regularly because I get to speak at various events and churches. People therefore assume I must carry some particular favour with God over and above 'ordinary' Christians. I had a lady approach me recently at the end of a seminar as I was packing up ready to leave. She told me that she hadn't actually been in my seminar because there was another more interesting one down the corridor, but she wondered whether I would pray for her! I did. She made to leave, then hesitated and turned back towards me. She asked, 'Did God by any chance say anything to you about me when you prayed?' I had to confess that he had not. I felt for her. I suspect she had come hotfoot from getting the speaker at the other seminar to pray for her, but didn't get what she wanted, so thought she'd try me as I was still there. She was clearly desperate to hear God's voice and thought that if she could get as many 'anointed' people as possible to pray for her, maybe God would speak to her through one of them. The truth, of course, is that I am no more special than she is. I carry no more favour with God than she does.

You cannot have a second-hand relationship with God. How do you think God feels when someone keeps going to the pastor or someone else, saying, 'Would you pray for me, would you ask God this and that for me?' What do you think God thinks? 'Hello, I'm your Dad, come and talk to me. I love you. You have the same access to me that the pastor does, so why won't you talk to me?'

There is, of course, a place for having someone to pray for you. In the passage above, the elders pray for someone who is sick and anoint him with oil. But only when he has done the things that God has said are his responsibility. Trying to get people to pray for us without first taking our God-given responsibility seriously will not work.

I do not any longer ask God to show me what the issues are in someone else's life. In a sense, wouldn't that be acting a little like a medium? The Bible is clear that Jesus is the only mediator between us and God (1 Timothy 2:5). Surely it would be far better for them to ask God to show *them*.

I am not saying that the Lord will never show you something about someone else. Sometimes he does. I always assume that if this happens it is primarily for my own information to help me to help them. I don't necessarily need to pass it on. I always handle it carefully because it's perfectly possible that I may have got it wrong.

The real problem is that so many people have come to believe that the answer lies in someone else praying for them or doing something else to them. It does not. I've learnt to put that responsibility back where it belongs – with the person seeking freedom. One leader told me that this simple concept – getting the person to pray first rather than going straight into praying for them – had made an enormous difference to their prayer ministry in that far fewer people were coming back time and again for prayer, because they had discovered how to resolve their issues.

I have known people who, looking back, acknowledge that they were addicted to being prayed for because it gave them a nice warm feeling. That is not the way to grow and bear fruit!

Churches that put too great an emphasis on simply praying for people without getting them to play their part usually end up with a much heavier pastoral burden, because they unwittingly send the message that a few 'special' people are the answer to people's issues – and of course they are not!

They need to assume responsibility for their own walk with the Lord

If you want to move on as a Christian and be spiritually healthy, no one else can do it for you. It's like being physically healthy. In order to improve your physical health, what would you do – look for a really healthy person and sit next to them in the hope that it would rub off on you? No, that would be ridiculous. If you want to be as healthy as they are, you will probably have to learn how they exercise, what they eat, how much rest they get – and then do the same. That's true spiritually too. If you find someone you perceive to be a spiritual giant and get them to pray for you, you will find that there is no magical transference of spirituality. But if you could be discipled by them, learn what they believe and believe the same, practise their spiritual disciplines, and persevere through trials and tribulations as they have, then you could mature as they have matured. But it starts when you assume your own responsibility.

We naturally tend to seek someone else out, of course, because we instinctively feel that we cannot do it on our own, that we are missing something. The truth, however, is this:

> *His divine power has given us* everything *we need for life and godliness through our knowledge of him who called us by his own glory and goodness.*   (2 PETER 1:3, EMPHASIS ADDED)

> *Praise be to the God and Father of our Lord Jesus Christ, who has blessed us in the heavenly realms with* every *spiritual blessing in Christ.*   (EPHESIANS 1:3, EMPHASIS ADDED)

We really do have everything we need. If anything is missing, it is our response to God in repentance and faith, which comes back to taking our God-given responsibility seriously.

Much as I would love to help a struggling person by confessing for them, repenting for them or forgiving for them, I simply can't. At first this seems like bad news if we have developed a 'quick fix' mentality and are hoping that God will send an 'anointed person' or step in dramatically. But actually this is great news!

Do you really want your spiritual maturity and growth as a disciple to be dependent on finding the right 'anointed' person to pray the right prayer? What if you never find the right person? Would it not be much better if it simply depended on you and God? That way nothing could get in the way of your becoming the person God has called you to be.

Guess what – that really is how it is. That is how God has set things up. Your spiritual growth and maturity do not depend on anyone else but you. You already have in Christ everything you need. You simply have to act on your own God-given responsibility, and nothing and no one can prevent you from becoming the person God wants you to be.

Principle 4

Listen to Your Emotions (They Are Trying to Tell You Something!)

Up to now I have been encouraging you to believe that what God says is true, whether it *feels* true or not. I may have given you the impression that emotions are a bad thing. It's time for me to redress the balance and have a look at what our emotions are for and how they can in fact be very helpful to us in our growth towards being fruitful disciples.

Did your mother used to brush your hair when you were a child? Did she ever do it when she was in a bad mood? Painful, wasn't it! It may not have felt like it at the time, but her emotional nature was a gift from God – honest!

Emotions are a warning system

Your emotions are part of your inner person and in many ways perform a similar function to the one performed by physical pain in your outer person (your physical body).

Wouldn't it be lovely if you could have some medical procedure that would take away your ability to feel physical pain? There was a child street-performer in Pakistan who had the ability to stick knives through his arms and walk on hot coals without feeling any pain. He and others in his family had genetic mutations that left them incapable of feeling pain. The good news is that, by studying their case, scientists are hopeful of being able to produce a new range of pain-killing treatments. The bad news, however, is that the lack of ability to feel pain has been much more of a curse than a blessing to the young performer and his family. According to one of the scientists who studied them, 'They would walk awkwardly and bump into things, as they didn't get hurt. They were covered in bruises. Life without pain sounds like a blessing, but it isn't.'[1] In fact, the performer died on his fourteenth birthday after jumping from a roof, possibly made braver by the fact that he knew that, whatever happened, it would not hurt.

The ability to feel physical pain is a gift from God for our own protection. It tells us, for example, when we are sitting too close to a hot fire, so that we can take corrective action and move further away. It alerts us to problems that require some form of action to alleviate them. A splinter must be removed before it turns septic and does us real damage. Constant headaches require medical investigation.

Your emotions perform a similar function. Wouldn't it be great if you never felt depressed, or anxious, or angry? No, it wouldn't. These emotions flare up from time to time and when they do, they are giving us important feedback to help us adjust. Just as feeling pain gives feedback to your body, emotions give feedback to your inner person.

Our emotions act as a warning system to alert us to areas of our belief system that are out of line with truth or 'how it is'. If we do not acknowledge our emotions, we can miss out on the important warnings they give us and fail to take corrective action, with potentially disastrous results. If, however, we acknowledge them, we can look at the area of truth they are alerting us to and do some work on it.

We have no direct control over our emotions

In our outer person (i.e. our physical bodies), there are some functions that we need to make a conscious decision to do

– for example, walking, eating, talking and so on. There are other functions of the body that happen completely automatically, prompted by areas of our brain that we do not directly control – for example, breathing, digestion and the beating of our hearts. If that did not happen, we could never sleep, otherwise we would die because our hearts would not beat and we would not breathe.

Dolphins work a little differently from us. Their heartbeat is automatic but they do have to control their breathing consciously. A dolphin has to think in advance about every breath it takes and decide to take it. That's logical because they spend most of their lives underwater and would not want to take a breath unless there were air to breathe in – and they don't have to breathe nearly as often as we do. It does, however, mean that they can never sleep because if they did, they would suffocate. They have an ingenious way around this – they only let half of their brain sleep at one time while the other half ensures that breathing and other functions, such as looking out for danger, continue. When one half has rested, the other half takes over the functions. That is why you may see a dolphin with just one eye open. He's not winking at you. It's just that the half of his brain that controls the other eye is sleeping!

Our inner person works in much the same way as our outer person. We have to make a conscious decision to do some things: to pray; to believe the truth; to forgive and so on. There are other things in our inner person, however, that we do not directly control. Our emotions fall into that category – we do not have direct control of them.

If you want to check that out, try this simple test. Think of someone you just do not like and decide that from now on you are going to like them. You will find that you just can't do it! The good news is that God doesn't expect us to be able to change our feelings like that. He does not ask us to *like* people – he commands us to *love* them, which is a choice we can make, not an emotion. We can choose to do what is right towards another person regardless of how we feel about them. If we make the effort to love them, we may well find that our emotions will eventually change and we will come to like them too.

And right there you have a key principle concerning our emotions: you cannot directly control them but you can change them over time as you make a conscious choice to heed their warning, believe the truth and act accordingly.

Emotions are determined by what we choose to believe

So, although we can't control them directly, in a general sense our emotions are the result of what we believe or choose to think, so we do have some influence over them. It is an influence that works over the long term rather than moment by moment.

Since the day we were born, the world, the flesh and the devil have been feeding us messages that are not in line with what is actually true. When we have bought into a lie that they have fed us, we have set ourselves up for some emotional problems because we will not see reality as it actually is. If, for example, we have bought into the lie that we are unlovable, we will tend to feel rejected by people even when they are not rejecting us at all. If our belief system does not reflect truth, then neither will our feelings.

Suppose your company is 'downsizing' and people are being laid off. On Monday morning you receive an e-mail from your boss asking to see you at 10.30 a.m. on Friday morning. Maybe your first reaction is anger: 'I've been here twenty years – they can't fire me!' Then anxiety: 'How am I going to pay the bills?' By Thursday you have convinced yourself you're going to lose your job and there's nothing you can do about it, so you are depressed. By Friday morning you are an emotional mess. With some trepidation you make your way to the boss's office and go in. To your surprise the whole board of the company is assembled there, then there's the sound of champagne corks popping and they say, 'Congratulations! We would like you to join the board.' How do you feel now? You probably faint!

The point is this. All week you've been going through a range of emotions – but none of them were based on reality. They were all based on how you perceived reality to be – but you were wrong.

Consider this Bible passage from Lamentations 3 where Jeremiah is at his wits' end. He clearly has a lot of physical and other problems and has come to the conclusion that God is the cause of them:

> I am the man who has seen affliction by the rod of his wrath. He has driven me away and made me walk in darkness rather than light; indeed, he has turned his hand against me again and again, all day long. He has made my skin and my flesh grow old and has broken my bones. He has besieged me and surrounded me with bitterness and hardship. He has made me dwell in darkness like those long dead. He has walled me in so I cannot escape; he has weighed me down with chains. Even when I call out or cry for help, he shuts out my prayer. He has barred my way with blocks of stone; he has made my paths crooked. Like a bear lying in wait, like a lion in hiding, he dragged me from the path and mangled me and left me without help… So I say, 'My splendour is gone and all that I had hoped from the Lord.'

Jeremiah's conclusion is devastating: 'My splendour is gone and all that I had hoped from the Lord.' Or, as The Message version of the Bible has it:

> I gave up on life altogether. I've forgotten what the good life is like. I said to myself, 'This is it. I'm finished. God is a lost cause.'

Take another look at the passage. Is this what God is really like? Would he really turn his hand against one of his servants again and again? Does he surround his people with bitterness and hardship? Does he shut out prayers? Of course not!

What was the problem? Simply that what Jeremiah believed about God wasn't actually true! God had not walled him in. God was not like a wild animal who had 'mangled' him. If your hope was in God and this was your belief about what he was like, you'd be depressed too!

Thankfully, Jeremiah does not leave it there. He thinks more about it and then he has a change in perspective, and the passage continues:

> *I remember my affliction and my wandering, the bitterness and the gall. I well remember them, and my soul is downcast within me. Yet this I call to mind and therefore I have hope: Because of the Lord's great love we are not consumed, for his compassions never fail. They are new every morning; great is your faithfulness. I say to myself, 'The Lord is my portion; therefore I will wait for him.'*

Everything changed internally for him when he said, in essence, 'Come on, Jeremiah, get a grip! Look at what is really true.' Then he wrote, 'This I call to mind and therefore I have hope. Great is your faithfulness.' What changed in his circumstances? Absolutely nothing. Did God change? No! The only thing that changed was in his mind: how he *looked* at his circumstances.

The battle we are in is a battle for truth and it takes place in our minds. The truth is that the circumstances of your life are not what determines who you are or what you feel – it's your perception of those circumstances.

The more we commit ourselves to the truth and choose to believe what God says is true, the more we will see our circumstances from God's perspective and the less our feelings will run away with us.

Changing how we feel

So the big question is: if we are overwhelmed by difficult circumstances from the past or in the present which cause us to be plagued by negative emotions, what can we do about it?

Let's look at a situation in the Bible which appeared to be overwhelming: the Israelite army versus the Philistine army (1 Samuel 17). The Philistines were saying, 'We don't want a bloodbath, why don't we just have our champions fight it out, winner take all?' Well, that was fine for them. They had a giant! No one could get anywhere near him in a sword fight – he seemed invincible.

The Israelite army was completely stressed out. But then a young man named David came along, said, 'How dare you challenge Almighty God?' and killed Goliath.

Both David and the Israelite army were confronted by exactly the same set of circumstances. It really is not the circumstances themselves that make the difference – it's how you see them. The Israelite army had not taken the whole of reality into account. They just saw the giant and themselves, rather as the Western worldview wants us to do. They had left God out of the picture. David, however, saw things as they really were. He knew that the almighty God, Creator of heaven and earth, was not only there but was on his side.

You are affected not so much by your environment and circumstances as by how you see your environment and circumstances. There is no time when God is not there. The God who has promised never to leave you or forsake you is working in every circumstance for your good (Romans 8:28).

David was doing what all of us are called to do. As the Bible often puts it, he was 'walking by faith'. We are not talking here about what some would call 'blind faith' – that is, a faith that is not based on anything more than wishful thinking. We are talking about acting on what God has said is true, how he says reality is. In other words, all that David did was recognize how the situation actually was and act accordingly.

When we are confronted with a situation that makes us feel overwhelmed or stresses us out, it is helpful to analyse what is actually happening. Is it the stressful situation that is causing us to feel overwhelmed? No – not directly. Our senses pick up what is happening in the world around us and pass the information to our brain. Our brain does not then immediately cause our body to go into a 'fight or flight' reaction to stress. First it passes the information via our mind and our mind interprets the data. That is what determines how we feel about it.

To use an analogy, our brain (which is part of our physical body) is like the hardware of a computer and our mind (which is part of our soul/spirit) is like the software. If your mind is 'programmed' differently from somebody else's – even though they face exactly the same set of circumstances – it will interpret them differently.

The main cause of depression is that we have come to believe through past experiences or failures that we are helpless or that there is no hope. We have learned a sense of helplessness and hopelessness because of what we have experienced. But is it true that we must feel helpless and hopeless today? It feels true but actually it is not. No Christian is helpless or hopeless.

Healing comes by changing that sense of helplessness and hopelessness, by 'changing the software' as we bring our belief system back in line with what is really true. That's what the Bible calls renewing your mind: understanding what is really true about God rather than what your experiences have caused you to believe; committing yourself to believe what God says is true even if it doesn't feel true.

How you feel is shaped not so much by actual events but by how you see them. If you want to be a balanced, whole person, you need to make sure that you are looking at them in a healthy way that reflects what is actually true.

Following feelings opens us up to attack

When we start training ourselves to see life as it really is, or in biblical terms, we start walking by faith, our emotions respond accordingly. We start by choosing to believe the truth, which works itself out in our behaviour. This then, over time, leads to a change in our feelings.

Immature Christians tend to act according to what they feel rather than what God says is true. If that's how you are, the enemy will have a field day when he condemns you. You'll tend to agree with him when he tells you that you are a 'no-good, miserable excuse for a Christian because you failed God yet again'. But the truth is that you are already forgiven and that God does not condemn you (Romans 8:1) – in fact he welcomes you to come boldly into his presence and he accepts you as his child.

Our emotions can actually lead to our giving the enemy a foothold in our lives if we do not handle them appropriately. Ephesians 4:26–27 says: '"In your anger do not sin": Do not let the sun go down while you are still angry, and do not give the devil a foothold.' Anger is an emotion, which means that we have no direct control over it. If something makes us angry, it makes us angry and that is that. That is why Paul makes clear that it is not in itself sinful ('In your anger do not sin'). However, if you dwell on your anger and let it turn into bitterness and unforgiveness, you will give the devil a foothold. This foothold is a position of influence in your thinking.

1 Peter 5:7–8 shows that anxiety can cause problems too if we do not handle it well. It starts with a well-known sentence that you may well have on a bookmark in your Bible or on a poster on your wall: 'Cast all your anxiety on him because he cares for you.' The passage continues with another couple of sentences that are just as well known: 'Be self-controlled and alert. Your enemy the devil prowls around like a roaring lion looking for someone to devour.' Even though it's likely that

you knew both of those passages well, I suspect that you did not realize that they follow one another directly. They are both part of the same idea. Peter is telling us that if we let anxiety get a grip of us, we are making ourselves much more vulnerable to the enemy's schemes against us.

If we don't handle emotions such as anger and anxiety in the right way, we are setting ourselves up for some problems. Satan is actively prowling around looking to take advantage of our emotions to get a foothold in our lives.

Learning to handle emotions well

We have said that our emotions are there to alert us to problems with our belief system. When we find ourselves caught in a state of anger, anxiety or depression, these emotions are flagging to us that we need to look at our belief system and see which parts are not in line with truth.

The best course of action would be to do just that. Most of us, however, tend to act in one of two other ways. We try either to ignore our emotions and stuff them down inside somewhere, or we do the opposite and let it all come out in one big splurge.

Ignoring emotions

We can consciously ignore our feelings or choose not to deal with them. I did something similar with a car I bought last year. Whenever I braked there was a curious scraping noise. However, having just spent out to buy the car, I wasn't about to spend any more on it. Eventually it got so bad that I was concerned for my safety and the car had to go into the garage. If I had taken it in earlier, apparently, just the brake pads would have had to be replaced. As it was, I had worn the discs too – a much more expensive job. That's how it is when we ignore our emotions – the longer we ignore them, the more damage it does us.

Consider how David felt when he lived in denial about sin: 'When I kept silent, my bones wasted away through my groaning all day long' (Psalm 32:3). When you consistently ignore what is going on inside, it will have an effect. It's important to be honest with God while we can, because if we bottle up our feelings too long, they will dominate our life.

Occasionally, I have come across people who have been badly hurt and have made a decision not to feel any more emotional pain. Sometimes they have made a vow never to cry again. It's very difficult to get them to connect with God because they won't be emotionally honest. The breakthrough comes when they start to acknowledge their feelings and let the tears come.

These people are usually suffering from various physical ailments. David said that when he kept quiet about his sins, his 'strength was sapped as in the heat of summer' (Psalm 32:4). Feelings don't die when you bury them, they are buried alive and they surface in some unhealthy way. It's like trying to bury a mole – it will just burrow its way up to the surface again.

Indiscriminate Expression

Another unhealthy way of responding to emotions is thoughtlessly to express everything you feel. The problem with indiscriminate expression is that it is not healthy for those around us. It may temporarily feel good to you – 'That's better. I just had to get that off my chest' – but it could be emotionally devastating for your spouse, children or friends.

> *Everyone should be quick to listen, slow to speak and slow to become angry, for man's anger does not bring about the righteous life that God desires.*   (JAMES 1:19–20)

We've already heard, 'In your anger do not sin' (Ephesians 4:26). How? Be like Jesus – get angry with sin, not with sinners. Turn over the tables, not the money changers.

Be honest

So what should we do when the warning light of our emotions comes on, when we feel angry, anxious or depressed? The healthy response is to be honest and acknowledge how we feel. Acknowledgment begins with God. Listen to David's 'prayer' for someone else:

> *Appoint an evil man to oppose him; let an accuser stand at his right hand. When he is tried, let him be found guilty, and may his prayers condemn him. May his days be few; may another take his place of leadership. May his children be fatherless and his wife a widow. May his children be wandering beggars; may they be driven from their ruined homes. May a creditor seize all he has; may strangers plunder the fruits of his labour. May no one extend kindness to him or take pity on his fatherless children. May his descendants be cut off, their names blotted out from the next generation. May the iniquity of his fathers be remembered before the Lord; may the sin of his mother never be blotted out. May their sins always remain before the Lord, that he may cut off the memory of them from the earth.*

(PSALM 109:6–15)

Did you know that that was in the Bible? Should it be? Well, it is the holy, inspired, perfect Word of God, and it does describe exactly how David felt. Have you ever felt like that? We all have. We've all been hurt, criticized, rejected and wanted revenge. But have you ever prayed like that? Would it be right to pray like that?

Well, David prayed like that, and God prompted him to write it down. Does God already know that you feel that way? Of course he does. God knows the thoughts and intentions of our hearts. All things are laid open and bare to him. So if God already knows it, why can't we be honest with him?

A lot of this is to do with our understanding of what God is like. Is he big enough to cope with an emotional outburst from us every now and then? Would he still be God, would he still love you, would you still be his child? Of course!

The difficulty of this Psalm, of course, is that it seems to be suggesting that I should ask God to bump someone off! But once David has had that emotional catharsis and been honest about how he feels, it all changes and he returns to praising God.

Jesus gave us an example of emotional honesty. He wept over the city of Jerusalem and at the grave of Lazarus. In the Garden of Gethsemane he said, 'My soul is overwhelmed with sorrow to the point of death' (Mark 14:34). Now if he felt the need to be expressive and honest like that, then I need to do that too.

God is our closest friend. We can be absolutely straight with him without fear of condemnation or rejection. He wants us to be honest. In fact, we can't really be right with him if we are not being honest with him. Sometimes he may have to bring us to the point of being honest to get us back into a right relationship with him.

Handling past traumas

We have been talking about managing day-to-day emotions, but what about major traumas from the past? All of us have had traumatic experiences that have scarred us emotionally and left us with emotional 'baggage' – a dreadful experience, the loss of a loved one, some form of abuse. These experiences are often deeply buried in our memories. We might be inno-cently watching something on TV or somebody might mention something in conversation that triggers the memories, and all the unpleasant feelings suddenly come flooding back, catching us unawares.

Quite understandably, people try to avoid events or people

that trigger those kinds of feelings: 'I am not going there if so and so is there'; 'I don't want to talk about that subject right now.' One lady was telling me that as a child she had been sexually abused. 'But,' she said, 'you can tell the Lord's dealt with it, can't you?' Actually, I wasn't sure I could, so I asked her to explain. 'Well,' she continued, 'the person who abused me was called Steve and in the past I'd have run from the room if I met someone called Steve.'

You can't avoid these triggers, especially if there are several. There is a much better way of dealing with them for a Christian. God doesn't want emotional pain from our past to influence us negatively today. He offers us complete resolution.

When you suffered negative experiences – violence, abuse, rejection or whatever – you mentally processed it at the time it happened. It almost certainly caused you to believe some things about God and yourself: 'I couldn't resist the abuse – I'm power-less, I'm a victim'; 'Those bullies told me I was rubbish – I guess I am'; 'My Dad never has time for me – I'm not important.'

For example, if you suffered some kind of sexual abuse as a child, at the time it happened you probably felt powerless, dirty or guilty. Those beliefs may well have stayed with you into adult life. If you thought God wasn't there for you, then you probably question God's love and your salvation. Even though the abuse no longer happens, you probably still feel powerless, dirty or guilty. But no Christian is powerless or dirty or guilty any more!

These things are simply strongholds in our minds, deeply rooted habitual patterns of thinking. They distort our under-standing of who we are and who God is. We remain in bond-age to the past, not because of what actually happened, but because of the lies we believed at the time. It's like that Land Rover driving across a muddy field day after day, making deep ruts. Those lies become like deep ruts in our minds. If we don't actively steer out of them by choosing truth, we will continue to live according to the same old flesh patterns.

Children of God are not primarily products of their past. We are primarily products of Christ's work on the cross and his resurrection. Nobody can change what happened, but we can be free from it. We can re-evaluate our past from the perspective of who we are now in Christ. All we are doing is looking at reality as it really is. From this truth perspective, God sets us free as we forgive from our hearts those people who have offended us.

The reason I can speak with confidence is that I have seen God bring resolution to deep emotional issues time after time. I've seen a young lady who for fourteen years struggled with anorexia, drug addiction and self-harm. Why? Because her past experiences were so painful that she had come to believe the lie that she was dirty, even though she was a Christian. As she went through The Steps To Freedom and then committed herself to believe what was really true, she changed. She now knows that she's clean through and through. The pain keeps diminishing. She's now helping other people find their freedom.

Another lady, who had experienced the worst imaginable kind of abuse as a child, also went through the Steps. I've seen her look again at what happened to her from the truth perspective of who she is now, and reject the lies she used to believe. Medical professionals had said they couldn't help her any more. Now she is whole and free in Christ. She too has helped many others find their freedom.

As I sit down with people I get to hear a lot of things that appal me, things that are practically unimaginable. But I see the Lord resolving them completely – not just helping people to cope, but bringing resolution. If I didn't see that, I don't think I could do it. The Lord delights in taking those who are pressed down and struggling, and making them fruitful.

If you have had particularly traumatic experiences in the past, you may need a mature Christian to help you as you renew your mind. They can support you as you work through painful memories, all the time reminding you that you are not a product of your past or a victim any more: you are a product of Christ's work on the cross. They can help you process your painful memories not from the perspective of who you were then but from the perspective of who you are now.

A word about mental illness

While we are looking at emotions, let's think briefly about the question of mental illness. I was speaking to a man recently who had a difficult set of circumstances and I was responding to his questions about how to start finding his way out of them. He had been diagnosed as 'clinically depressed'. I am sure the diagnosis was correct. To him the diagnosis had been something of a relief in that he now had a label for his powerful negative feelings. However, from where I was sitting, it looked as if there was a distinct danger that it would have a negative effect in that he seemed almost to have taken that label as part of his identity. In thinking of himself, fairly high on his list of attributes would be 'clinically depressed', as if it was something inevitable that could never change.

Talking to him, it was fairly clear to me that his depression was rooted in past experiences that had taught him to believe that he was hopeless. That, of course, is absolutely not true. As he learns to replace those lies with truth, he has every expectation of coming out of that depression. He simply needs to learn to interpret the data of his current circumstances in the light of how things really are rather than according to what his past experiences have taught him.

In grappling with this issue, we need to bear in mind that we have both an inner person (our soul/spirit) and an outer person (our body). In the analogy we used earlier, we noted that the brain functions like the hardware of a computer and the mind is like the software that runs on it. Hardware on its own cannot accomplish much. It needs software to make it useful.

In the Western worldview, there is no scientific concept of the mind being distinct from the brain, so the first reaction when someone reports a problem in their thinking is that there must be some problem with the brain. Can there be? Of course. Alzheimer's disease is a common brain disorder. Bipolar disorder ('manic depression') is another.

In other words, in the Western world, when there is a mental and emotional problem, the emphasis is put on the hardware. But in the Bible the overwhelming emphasis is not on the hardware, it's on the software. It's on the mind: choosing truth, believing the truth, taking every thought captive and so on. The computer cannot function any other way than how it has been programmed.

If a particular case of mental illness is caused by a physical problem, then the appropriate course of action would be to see a medical specialist and at the same time pray for physical healing. If, however, it is caused by a fault in the belief system, a better course of action by far would be to rectify the faulty thinking.

How can you tell whether it is a hardware or software issue? Most of us, myself included, are simply not qualified to say. If a Christian came to me with some mental and emotional issues, I would suggest that they go first of all to the Lord and ask him to show them where they need to repent and believe the truth (in the way we will look at in the next section of this book). It is difficult to see how repenting and believing the truth could do anyone any harm. The worst thing that could happen is that they would be in great shape for church on Sunday morning! If that did not work, I would suggest that they go to their doctor.

In the early days of Freedom In Christ Ministries, we were contacted by Chris, a Christian living in a remote part of Wales who had been diagnosed as paranoid schizophrenic. He had an abusive past and had been caught up in drug addiction and pornography.

'Schizophrenia' is a label used by medical professionals to describe a set of symptoms. It does not tell us a great deal about the cause of the symptoms. One of the possible symptoms is that the sufferer hears voices, and that was certainly the case with Chris. When he told us what the voices were saying, it sounded to me just like the accusation of the enemy: it was lies about God being angry with him and how he would lose his salvation. On one occasion, the voices were telling him to blaspheme the name of Jesus and that if he did that, he would lose his salvation. They were so insistent that Chris knew he would eventually do as they said just to silence them. He decided to take evasive action. His mother had to physically prevent him from cutting out his tongue with a knife.

Chris himself believed the voices were not due to a physical fault in his brain but were due to demonic activity. His own church leader refused to entertain a discussion on the possibility of there being a demonic issue – it was outside of his experience and he was frightened. In the end Chris bought a set of our conference tapes and a copy of The Steps To Freedom In Christ and took himself through the process. He has since listened to the tapes countless times to get hold of who he is in Christ and to understand the victory he has over Satan – it was key for Chris to understand that he did not just have to put up with the voices but, assuming they were demonic, he had authority over them.

In the early days he needed lots of reassurance. Nowadays he gets in touch occasionally simply to encourage us – and encourage us he does. A couple of years ago he reported that his psychiatrist was astonished at the progress he had made and he has not looked back. He has nearly completed a course to become a lay preacher; he is overcoming his agoraphobia; and he regularly visits people in the psychiatric institutions he used to be in and leads them to the Lord and to freedom.

In this case, it seems to me that Chris was right – he was up against the demonic. Once footholds of the enemy were removed and Chris renewed his mind, the problem went away. In other cases where schizophrenia has been diagnosed, the symptoms may have some other cause. I am simply not qualified to say. I am, however, haunted by one thing Chris says to me all the time: 'You know, Steve, I see all these people in the hospital where I spent years and they are just like I was. I know that Jesus can set them free but all that is happening is that they are being drugged out of their minds to keep them quiet because that's the only thing the doctors can do to help.'

If the thought of people hearing voices in their mind disturbs you, bear in mind that it is something that health professionals see all the time. For most of them, however, their worldview precludes the possibility that it could be caused by anything other than an abnormality in the brain. Look at the world the way God says it is, however, with spiritual reality, and a lot more possibilities are opened up. In fact, in my experience many Christians hear voices in their mind that they do not recognize as their own. They just don't like to tell anyone about it because others might assume they are suffering from a mental illness. When they understand that Satan is quite capable of putting voices into their mind and that they can do something about it, it (quite literally!) puts their mind at rest.

We need to be careful to take a balanced view of reality, steering a middle path between one extreme of seeing demons as the cause of every problem and the other of ignoring the reality of the spiritual world. Let's recognize both that there is real mental illness caused by a failure of the hardware and that it is perfectly possible that footholds given to the enemy through sin are involved. And above all, let's remember that whatever the cause, there is no one who is unloved by God or who cannot become everything that God is calling them to be.

NOTE
1. Quoted in *The Times*, 14 December 2006.

PART 2

Resolving the Effects of the Past

We can start to look now at how practically we can resolve the effects of the past and go on to walk in freedom.

There are two things we need to do. First of all, we need to resolve any personal and spiritual conflicts that might be holding us back. This is a little like a computer checking for viruses – things that are hidden that can stop it performing as it should do.

Then we need to renew our minds because, according to Paul in Romans 12:2, that is how we can be transformed. If we try renewing our minds without first doing the 'virus check', however, we are unlikely to get very far.

Let's remind ourselves of Jesus' 'manifesto' from Isaiah 61:

> *The Lord has anointed me to preach good news to the poor. He has sent me to bind up the broken-hearted, to proclaim freedom for the captives and release from darkness for the prisoners.*

And also let's remember two of the reasons why he came:

'I have come that they may have life, and have it to the full.'
(JOHN 10:10)

The reason the Son of God appeared was to destroy the devil's work. (1 JOHN 3:8)

In talking of resolving the effects of the past where a Christian – one who is a new creation – is concerned, we are not talking simply about giving them strategies to cope or a 'workaround'. We are talking about seeing complete resolution of those issues in Christ so that they can live in the reality of their new identity and become everything God wants them to be instead of being defined and held back by past experiences.

Resolve Personal and Spiritual Conflicts

When we commit ourselves to truth, increasingly we learn to see the world as it really is. However, we are in a battle for truth that takes place in our minds and the reality is that, unless we take back ground that has previously been given to the enemy through sin, it is difficult for us to make real, lasting connections with the truth.

Resolving personal and spiritual conflicts is absolutely crucial but so often overlooked by those brought up with the Western worldview, because it does not sit comfortably within it. In the last few years I have been amazed as thousands of churches have taken up and used The Freedom In Christ Discipleship Course written by Neil Anderson and myself to help tens of thousands of Christians become fruitful disciples. The course contains much the same teaching as this book series as well as a 'ministry component'. About two thirds of the way through, all participants are encouraged to go through The Steps To Freedom In Christ. This is a tool that Christians can use to take back any ground that has been given to the enemy by resolving personal and spiritual conflicts.

I have been dismayed to hear that some churches (thankfully a small minority) loved the teaching sessions in the course but have not seen the need to take people through The Steps To Freedom In Christ. They have fallen for the Western worldview which predisposes us to think that good teaching alone is all that is needed for people to know the truth. Although some people are impacted and changed simply by hearing the truth of who they now are in Christ, the reality is that, if we leave in place the means the enemy has of interfering with our thinking, over time that gain is likely to be eroded. For others, although they may enjoy the sessions and appreciate the teaching, if they do not then go on to close doors open to the enemy to influence their minds, it is unlikely to have any lasting effect.

What are these personal and spiritual conflicts? As we have seen, Ephesians 4:26–27 says: '"In your anger do not sin": Do not let the sun go down while you are still angry, and do not give the devil a foothold.' If we allow anger to lead us into sin, we give the devil a 'foothold' in our life. That word 'foothold' is *topos* in Greek and literally means a 'place'. If Satan can lead us into sin, he can gain a 'place', a point of influence in our lives. In terms of the battle for the mind, he gains some influence in our thinking. Those footholds seem to give him the ability to blind us to truth in much the same way as he blinds the minds of unbelievers (see 2 Corinthians 4:4).

That is the reason why we sometimes simply cannot grasp truth or hold on to it, why it seems to slip through our fingers. I remember the first time this was brought home to me. I was taking someone through The Steps To Freedom who looked like a normal, educated person with good eyesight. When I asked them to read the opening prayer, they stared at it for some time and declared that they could not read the words on the page. What was happening? Spiritual interference. There were so many points of influence for the enemy in that person's mind, that he was using them as best he could to prevent the process taking place. He was ultimately unsuccessful, of course, and at the end of the process, just to demonstrate the difference, I got them to read the prayer again, which, of course, was something they could do very easily once they had resolved the outstanding issues.

How are those issues resolved? Very simply and undramatically. The process is based on James 4:7: 'Submit to God. Resist the devil and he will flee from you.' During The Steps To Freedom, you start by asking the Holy Spirit to show you any footholds that the enemy has in your life through past sin. As he shows you, you choose to repent and renounce and, because your power and authority in Christ is much greater than the enemy's, his right to influence you is taken away.

Having submitted to God, at the end of the process you command the enemy to leave your presence. Because you have dealt with the issues that the Holy Spirit has revealed to you, the enemy will have no option but to flee from you.

It is a kind and gentle process. You are in control and the outcome is in your hands. It's just between you and God. If you deal with everything the Holy Spirit shows you, at the end of the process you will be free in Christ. The Steps don't set you free, Jesus Christ does.

The Steps is simply a tool to help you cover the whole of your life history in one comprehensive session. It is something that I try to do once a year – it always amazes me how much rubbish I can accumulate in that time!

If you want to use The Steps as a tool in your own life, the best way to do that is in the context of your own church as part of The Freedom In Christ Discipleship Course. If that is not possible, it is possible to go through it on your own. A Steps To Freedom In Christ DVD (Monarch, 2004) is available to guide you through. Alternatively, Neil Anderson's book *Restored* (Monarch, 2007) is a way of going through on your own. I recommend, however, that if you possibly can, you find a mature Christian friend to be alongside you as you go through it, and ideally another friend to be there to pray. They won't do the work for you – it's still between you and God – but in my experience having them there really helps you go much deeper.

The Freedom In Christ Discipleship Course lasts thirteen weeks. Do you know how long the early church spent discipling new converts? Three years! Most of that time was spent helping them deal with the kinds of issues that are covered in The Steps To Freedom. I would hate to think that people would treat this as some kind of one-off 'programme' that they can go through and say 'Been there, done that.' The real benefit comes when

Christians get hold of the principles behind The Steps and take them deep into their lives so that taking hold of freedom and standing in it simply become part of how we live.

The Steps is an opportunity to put everything on the table before God at one time and ask him to reveal anything that the enemy might be able to use to hold us back. Let's run through the areas covered by The Steps to see what sort of sin can give ground to the enemy. I'll cover most briefly. The one I will spend most time on is the one that we have noticed tends to be the major issue for most Western Christians.

The occult and idols

The enemy may well have tempted you in the past to take part in an occult practice, often as 'a bit of fun'. However, in participating in that, no matter how it was dressed up, you were asking for guidance from the enemy. In the Old Testament, this was seen as such a serious issue that people who gave false guidance were to be stoned to death, and those who consulted them also faced stiff measures. There are similar warnings about false teachers and false prophets in the New Testament.

The issue at stake in the Steps is not your salvation but your fruitfulness as a Christian. Remember that you are in a battle against one who cannot do anything about the fact that you now belong to Christ but who can attempt to make you a spiritual casualty, a Christian who does not bear fruit. Satan will use any means he can to hold you back. If he can find a way to influence your thinking, he will.

Some think that if something happened a long time ago, it cannot be of consequence now in the present. That is not the case. Imagine the enemy as a bent lawyer scrutinizing your past life with a magnifying glass, looking for any loophole he can find to get the influence he is looking for. It's a bit like

what sometimes happens in the political arena when someone puts themselves forward to run for a high-profile post.
Immediately their political enemies and some elements of the
media start raking over their past to see what dirt they can find
to hold them back. What you are doing in The Steps process is
denying the enemy any possibility of finding a way to hold you
back by resolving anything he may come up with.

In each of these areas, you start by asking the Holy Spirit
to bring to your mind any unresolved sin that might allow the
enemy to hold you back by influencing your thinking. In this
first step, the Holy Spirit may bring to your mind an occasion
when you participated in using the ouija board as a bit of a
game at school. Is that really a problem? Well, if you asked the
Holy Spirit to show you what the issues are and that came to
your mind, it would be wise to assume that he has done just
that and it is a problem. However, it really is straightforward
to sort it out. You simply need to say something like, 'I confess
using the ouija board and I renounce it and take away any
ground the enemy gained in my life.' There is a prayer to use
in The Steps book. Can just saying a few words really have
any effect? If you mean them, they certainly can. Why? It's
not the power of the words themselves so much as the power
and authority of the one saying them – you are a child of God
seated with Christ at the right hand of the Father! Your word
carries weight.

This is similar to the way the early church acted. They
would encourage people to say, 'I renounce you, Satan, and
all your works and all your ways.' They would then specifically renounce every counterfeit religious experience they had,
every false vow or pledge they made, and every false teacher or
doctrine in which they believed.

We also need to look at our priorities and identify areas
in our life that have become more important to us than God.
These are called 'idols'. Originally, the word referred to the false
gods that the Old Testament Israelites were tempted to worship, but our modern usage of the term is not so different.

Why were the Israelites tempted to worship Baal, a god of the Canaanites, for example? Because he was a fertility god and promised abundance in their crops as well as an opportunity for lust in fertility ceremonies. Is that so different from the idols we are tempted to worship, such as material goods, money and sex? The major difference, perhaps, is that it is easier for us to deceive ourselves that there isn't a problem.

Committing ourselves to truth

We are in a battle for truth. It is a battle between the father of lies (John 8:44) and the Spirit of Truth (John 16:13) and it takes place in our mind. We have already seen the importance of committing ourselves to truth. This needs to be an ongoing attitude.

Satan's strategies against us are essentially three fold. He can tempt us, he can accuse us and he can deceive us. Of the three, deception is by far the most powerful because if we are deceived, by definition we do not realize it.

It is not just Satan who sets out to deceive us. The world and the flesh have been doing that ever since we were born. We can also deceive ourselves.

The trouble is that deception, by definition, feels like truth. In a way the whole of The Steps process is about truth and lies. Most people come out of it with the ability to identify for the first time lies they have been believing, and with a strategy to renew their minds.

Forgiving others

This is the area I want to deal with more thoroughly because, in my experience, very few of us have understood what forgiveness really is and why we are commanded to do it.

If you forgive anyone, I also forgive him. And what I have forgiven – if there was anything to forgive – I have forgiven in the sight of Christ for your sake, in order that Satan might not outwit us. For we are not unaware of his schemes.

(2 CORINTHIANS 2:10–11)

If you want to see demonic activity in the Western church, the place to look would be in division among Christians. In my experience nothing keeps you in bondage to the past more than an unwillingness to forgive. Nothing gives Satan greater opportunity to stop a church growing than roots of bitterness, unforgiveness, and backbiting.

Think for a minute: what is the worst thing that anyone ever did to you? Have you got something specific? Now, ask yourself, 'Why should I forgive that person?'

God tells you to forgive

The blunt answer is quite simply because God commands you to. 'Forgive as the Lord forgave you' (Colossians 3:13).

But he is not asking us to do anything that he himself has not done – and at immense, unimaginable cost. All God is asking us to do is to put our relationship with others on the same basis as he has put his relationship with us. We must learn to relate to others on the same basis that God relates to us. 'Freely you have received, freely give' (Matthew 10:8). The implication is that we cannot have a righteous relationship with God if we do not have a righteous relationship with other people.

However, simply being told that God commands us to forgive does not necessarily help. We have a righteous sense of indignation about what was done to us and we want to see justice done. We want the perpetrator to pay.

Although we understand God's command to forgive, it can feel as if we simply cannot do it. In fact, that's not the case. God is not the kind of God who would ask us to do something that we could not – that would be cruel. If he is asking us to do something, it is by definition possible. As Paul says, 'I can do everything through him who gives me strength' (Philippians 4:13).

Forgiveness sets us free

Jesus taught the principles of forgiveness very clearly using an illustration in Matthew 18:21–35. It was sparked by this important question from Peter:

> Then Peter came to Jesus and asked, 'Lord, how many times shall I forgive my brother when he sins against me? Up to seven times?' Jesus answered, 'I tell you, not seven times, but seventy-seven times.'

I wonder what had just happened. I get the impression that someone – probably one of the other disciples – was really getting up Peter's nose through some irritating thing they kept doing. He knew he had to forgive but surely he didn't have to keep on and on forgiving... Did he?

I wonder if he was tempted, once he had heard Jesus' response, to start recording every time the other person committed the sin against him until he got up to seventy-eight times, at which point he could say, 'Right, I've been waiting for this moment. Step outside – I'm going to punch you on the nose!' I suspect not. I'm sure he understood that Jesus was saying he needed to keep on forgiving.

That, of course, does not feel like a very satisfactory answer to one who really wants to see justice done and to get revenge. So Jesus goes on to set out his illustration:

> Therefore, the kingdom of heaven is like a king who wanted to settle accounts with his servants. As he began the settlement, a man who owed him ten thousand talents was brought to him. Since he was not able to pay, the master ordered that he and his wife and his children and all that he had be sold to repay the debt.

Do you know what it's like to have a debt that you can't pay? I do. In my business life at one time everything collapsed and the debts piled up and there were nasty legal letters and court orders. I couldn't find a way out. I usually enjoy work but I went though a period of six to nine months when I would have to answer my wife's usual question of 'Did you have a good day?' with a 'Not really.' Owing money you can't pay feels awful. It needed a miracle and actually the Lord did one.

Jesus deliberately chooses an impossibly large debt here. Ten thousand talents was a huge sum, way beyond a lifetime's earnings for most people. A talent was roughly equivalent to £500 (or 1,000 US dollars) in today's terms. So you are looking at £5 million or $10 million. What Jesus is trying to show is that there is no way this man could hope to repay the debt.

Your debt to God was taken by Jesus and ripped up. How large was it?

Wouldn't it be easy to compare ourselves to others and think, 'Well, my life hasn't been that bad. I've got nowhere near as much to be forgiven for as that other person has'? The truth is that we simply cannot grasp just how holy and right-eous God is – it is so far beyond our experience. Our very best efforts are like a dirty rag before God (Isaiah 64:6). Without Christ, we all stand condemned. Just like this servant, we all need to be forgiven a huge sum that we cannot possibly pay ourselves.

The servant fell on his knees before him. 'Be patient with me,' he begged, 'and I will pay back everything.'

There was no way he could do this – both he and the master knew it. In the same way, there is no way you or I could repay our debt to God – it was incalculable.

God is just. That means that he is fair. But if he treated us with justice and gave us what we deserved, we would all end up in hell. Thankfully, God is also merciful and he found a way to forgive and accept us without compromising the requirement for justice. The punishment we deserved fell at unimaginable cost on Christ. When someone exercises mercy, they are making a decision not to give people what they deserve. We are told to be merciful to others as God has been merciful to us (Luke 6:36). In other words, we are not to give people what they deserve.

But God goes even further than that. He did not just take the punishment that is rightfully ours on himself so that we are off the hook. He actually showers us with good things as well. That is giving us what we don't deserve, or what the Bible calls 'grace'.

This is the basis that God has established for his relationship with us. We are to relate to other people in exactly the same way. We are not to give people what they deserve. In fact, we are to give them what they don't deserve, which is what the master did for the servant:

> The servant's master took pity on him, cancelled the debt and let him go. But when that servant went out, he found one of his fellow-servants who owed him a hundred denarii.

A denarius is a day's wages – so this is three months' wages. You can work out what that would mean for your household budget. This is not a trivial debt but it is much less than the one he himself had been let off.

> He grabbed him and began to choke him. 'Pay back what you owe me!' he demanded. His fellow-servant fell to his knees and begged him, 'Be patient with me, and I will pay you back.' But he refused. Instead, he went off and had the man thrown into prison until he could pay the debt. When the other servants saw what had happened, they were greatly distressed and went and told their master everything that had happened. Then the master called the servant in. 'You wicked servant,' he said, 'I cancelled all that

debt of yours because you begged me to. Shouldn't you have had mercy on your fellow-servant just as I had on you?' In anger his master turned him over to the jailers to be tortured, until he should pay back all he owed.

The servant had been completely forgiven an enormous debt even though he did not deserve it. Yet when he was put in the position of the one being owed money (even though it was a much smaller debt), he refused point blank to forgive it. Unsurprisingly, when the master got to hear about it, he was furious. He turned him over to the jailers to be tortured until he paid back what he owed.

Jesus then finishes his illustration with one of the most chilling statements recorded in the Gospels:

This is how my heavenly Father will treat each of you unless you forgive your brother from your heart.

Read that through a couple of times and let it sink in. How will our heavenly Father treat us if we do not forgive from the heart? A literal translation of Jesus' words would be: 'his master turned him over to the tormentors'.

The word Jesus used for 'tormentors' often refers to spiritual torment in the New Testament. It is the same word the demon used in Mark 5:7 when it said to Jesus, 'Swear to God that you won't torment me!' It is the word used to describe what will happen to Satan and his cohorts in the end: 'They will be tormented day and night for ever and ever' (Revelation 20:10).

This is where we begin, perhaps, to understand that the main reason God commands us to forgive is for our own good, for our own freedom. Jesus warns that, if we do not forgive from our hearts, we will suffer spiritual torment. This amounts to much the same thing as opening a door to the enemy's influence in your life. After all, refusing to forgive when God has commanded you to forgive is sin, and sin gives the enemy a foothold.

If you know someone who has been locked in bitterness and unforgiveness for years, you can usually see evidence of this torment in their faces. In a conference situation, I can sometimes pick out people affected by this just by looking at them. Often my instincts are confirmed when I get a chance to talk to them. This is not any kind of spiritual discernment. It's just that the torment really does start to show.

Forgiving from the heart

In order to avoid that torment, Jesus says we need to forgive from the heart. What does it mean to forgive from the heart? It's simply being emotionally honest about what was done to us and just how much it hurt us and how wrong it was. It certainly doesn't mean saying a quick 'I forgive so and so' and thinking it is dealt with. If we are truly going to forgive, we have to face the pain and the hate that we feel. We have to be honest with God.

In The Steps To Freedom, it is recommended that we use this formula: 'Lord, I choose to forgive (name the person) for (what they did or failed to do) which made me feel (verbally tell the Lord every hurt and pain he brings to your mind)'. People are encouraged to be emotionally honest by telling God every hurt they remember and staying with it until they are sure it has all been put on the table. We have to let God lead us to the emotional core where the healing is going to take place.

I am not pretending that this is not painful or difficult. It is. However, this is not some kind of pointless exercise. It is done in order to resolve – completely resolve – this issue and get rid of the pain that we have been carrying around with us. We cannot move on from the past until we forgive.

It is for your sake that you forgive. 'But you don't know how much that hurt me.' Don't you see that they are still hurting you? How do you stop the pain? By forgiving.

Once a lady came up to me after I had been teaching on this subject. She explained that her husband had left her for someone else. That is painful – and I don't want to trivialize it in any way. She said, 'I'm not ready to forgive him yet.' She's effectively saying, 'By staying angry, I'm getting my own back on him.' Her ex is probably travelling round the world, going to parties, having a good time. The fact that she is sitting there resentful, bitter and angry does hurt someone. But not him – her!

I used to go fishing a lot. Once I walked behind another fisherman who was doing a rather flamboyant cast and ended up with a fish hook in my cheek, complete with a couple of wriggling maggots. It wasn't my fault. It was his – he was the one who was not paying attention. But I was connected to the other fisherman via his hook and line, and it was hurting *me*. How could I get rid of the pain? By leaving the hook in place? No. By taking it out!

We think that by forgiving someone we let them off the hook – but by not forgiving them we stay hooked to the pain and the past. We are the ones with the hook in us!

Understanding what forgiveness is and what it is not

An issue between us and God

One of the key things we need to understand is that the real issue when it comes to forgiveness is not so much between us and the other person. It is between us and God because he is the one who commands us to forgive.

We do not even have to go to the other person in order to forgive them. In fact, the process does not involve them at all – it is between us and God alone. Jesus did say (Matthew 5:23–24) that if we go to church and remember that somebody has something *against us*, we should leave our offering and go to that person to be reconciled. Yes, if you have offended someone else, go to that person, ask for forgiveness and put things right if you can. But if someone has offended you, you don't go to them, you go to God. Your need to forgive others is first and foremost an issue between you and God. If you think about it, there is logic in that because your freedom cannot be dependent on other people – otherwise it could not be guaranteed.

After you have forgiven, you may be reconciled to the other person. On the other hand, you may not – it does not depend just on you. But whether you are reconciled or not, you will have removed the enemy's ability to hold you back.

Not tolerating sin

Does God forgive? He certainly does. Does he tolerate sin? Absolutely not. That would go against his character. Forgiveness does not mean that we tolerate sin.

This is most difficult when someone is in a situation where they are being sinned against continually – for example, a wife who is being physically abused by her husband. In the past, some churches in effect advised abused children and wives to 'Go home and be submissive.' The Bible certainly tells wives to be submissive but that's not all it says. 1 Peter 2:13–18 and Romans 13:1–7 instruct us to submit to the governing authorities whom God has placed in authority over us. They have put laws in place to protect that wife. It is perfectly possible to forgive someone yet still decide to turn them over to the authorities to let the law take its course. The fact is that that kind of abuse tends to run in a cycle that simply goes on and on until someone puts a stop to it.

I've seen this in action. I work with someone who suffered years of abuse from the hands of her father. It caused her great difficulties in her life – almost insurmountable ones. But she found her freedom in Christ and she forgave her father. However, at the same time she turned him in to the police because she was aware that he was coming into contact with children and she was concerned that he might be a danger. She achieved her aim of getting him put on the sex offenders' register and making sure that the parents of those children were aware. Through all that she managed to maintain a relationship with him because she had forgiven him from the heart. She was free.

A lady told me that her Christian husband kept having affairs. She continually forgave him and thought that part and parcel of that was that she should take him back and act as if nothing had happened. He kept on having affairs. I advised her to forgive him but then draw a line in the sand and say that if he did it one more time, he must leave. That is not inconsistent with forgiving him. To be honest, you feel a little nervous when you give that kind of advice. I first met the husband when they both came to a Freedom In Christ conference. He took me aside and thanked me and told me that the line in the sand was the wake-up call he needed to get his act together and sort his life out.

You have every right to put a stop to sin by laying down biblical guidelines, or by removing yourself from a particular situation. That is not at all inconsistent with forgiveness. You can forgive while at the same time refusing to put up with more abuse.

Not sweeping what was done under the carpet

For many this is the missing piece of the jigsaw. They have come to understand that to forgive someone is to say in effect that what was done somehow did not matter. But it did matter. Very much.

In no way is God asking you to sweep what was done under the carpet as if it did not matter. In fact, quite the opposite. He promises that if you entrust the matter to him, he will ensure that it is not swept under the carpet.

The main reason we will not let go of what has been done to us is because we want to see it put right. We want to see justice done. We want revenge. Look carefully at what God says to this:

Do not take revenge, my friends, but leave room for God's wrath, for it is written: 'It is mine to avenge; I will repay,' says the Lord.
(ROMANS 12:19)

When you forgive, although you are letting the person off your hook, you are not letting them off God's hook. When you choose to forgive, you are taking a step of faith to trust God to be the righteous judge who will make everything right in the end by demanding full payment for everything done against you. Nothing will be swept under the carpet. God really will demand justice for everything that has been done against you. Everyone who sinned against you will have to stand before God and explain it – either it will be paid for by the blood of Christ if the person is a Christian, or they will have to face the judgment of God if they are not. 'I will repay' – God will settle every account some day.

You can hand all of that pain and those demands for justice and revenge over to God, safe in the knowledge that he will repay. Justice will be done. In the meantime you can walk free of it.

Of course, that is not to say that the consequences of what was done can always be changed. When we forgive we have to come to terms with that and agree to live with the consequences of someone else's sin. That is not fair – but we have no choice. We will have to do it anyway. The only choice we have is whether we do it in freedom or bitterness.

Conversely, some spend time worrying about whether what was done to them really was wrong. They wonder whether they misunderstood or think of some other reason why the person might have been justified in what they did. I always try to discourage people from thinking that way. In fact, forgiveness is not primarily about objective right and wrong. It's about clearing rubbish out of your life and walking away from it. If you felt offended, you need to forgive whether or not the person was actually in the wrong.

When people go through The Steps we suggest that they consider whether they need to forgive God. Of course, from an objective point of view God has done nothing wrong – he is perfect. However, it's perfectly possible for us to feel that he has done wrong to us – perhaps we had been praying for someone to get better and they died; maybe we cannot understand why he let circumstances unfold as they did. If we have felt offended by God, even though we recognize intellectually that he has not acted wrongly, we need to release those feelings. If you feel uncomfortable saying, 'I forgive you, God', you could say something like, 'I release my feelings of hurt against you, God'.

We also suggest that they consider forgiving themselves. Many people so regret things they did in the past and bad choices they made that they will not let them go. They forgive other people but they will not forgive themselves. When they finally make that choice to forgive themselves, they are simply catching up with the reality that God has already completely forgiven them and made them new creations in Christ.

I received this letter from someone who was taken through The Steps To Freedom In Christ:

> We were led into a quiet time coming before God with a list of people we wanted to forgive. The Lord took me back to a time of great pain. Forty-one years ago I had a baby girl and was made to give her up for adoption. I had always blamed myself for not being strong enough to fight for her and keep her. As I was re-living this time in my mind the Lord asked me to forgive myself. I told Him I didn't know how to do this, it didn't seem enough to say the words.
>
> The Lord then gave me a picture of the baby lying in a crib beside me; she even had a little bonnet on. He asked me to lift her out and put her into His arms, saying she was His and He would care and look after her always and now I could forgive myself.

I did as He asked and I know, without fully understanding, that a huge chain has been broken in the spiritual realms. God has given me freedom from the heavy guilt I had carried.

A choice, not a feeling

I was speaking to someone after a conference recently who was completely chewed up by unforgiveness and knew it. He wanted to be free. He kept saying, 'Yes, I think I will forgive.' I said, 'Well, why don't you do it now?' He didn't think he could. I eventually realized that he was imagining that at some point in the future a 'feeling of forgiveness' would come over him and he would be able to forgive. I told him that if he was waiting for that to happen, he would be waiting a long time. We never feel like forgiving. I explained that forgiveness was not an emotion but a decision. You make a choice to forgive. You don't need to wait for anything else to happen first. You simply choose. When he understood that, he took a deep breath and there and then made the choice. 'I feel so much better already,' was the first thing he said after forgiving.

As with everything else, when we choose to act according to the truth, our feelings will eventually fall into line. Try it the other way round, and you'll get nowhere.

Rebellion

What would you do if you discovered that someone in your church was a practising witch? That would be an interesting question for your leaders – I dare say that they would not ignore the matter.

What would you do if you discovered that someone in your church was rebellious – for example, criticizing leaders, refusing to follow those whom God had placed in leadership roles? That is possibly an even more interesting question because you may well be able to think of people like that in your church already!

Here is an interesting verse in that context: 'For rebellion is the same as witchcraft' (1 Samuel 15:23). In God's eyes, rebellion and witchcraft are pretty much the same thing, certainly in their degree of seriousness. It's worth reading that verse through a few more times and pondering it. Because it does not seem to us as if witchcraft and rebellion are on a par. But God says they are.

The reason that rebellion may not seem that serious to us is because our view is easily coloured by the world and, in our society, rebellion is the norm. There is a general lack of respect for those in government, for example, yet the Bible is clear that God established all governing authorities and requires us to be submissive (Romans 13:1–5; 1 Peter 2:13–17). Christians are often as guilty as the rest of society in harbouring a rebellious spirit.

Of course, those who overstep the bounds of their authority do not have to be obeyed. We need to submit only to authorities that act within their God-given boundaries. However, when they are doing that, our responsibility is to submit, whether we agree with them or not.

When you choose to submit to a law that you regard as nonsensical (a speed limit, perhaps), or a wife chooses to submit to a husband whom she knows is quite a lot less than perfect, it is an act of faith in God. We are trusting God to protect us. He does not simply want us to submit outwardly but is looking for a sincere submission from the heart to those he has placed in authority over us.

When I think of submission I think back to when I was a child, and I used to have mock wrestling fights with my father. When I had had enough I had to shout 'I submit!' In other words, 'I submit' was an admission of failure, of weakness. But for Christians submission is always a choice. God never forces us to do it. The ultimate example of a life of submission is Jesus himself:

During the days of Jesus' life on earth, he offered up prayers and petitions with loud cries and tears to the one who could save him from death, and he was heard because of his reverent submission. (HEBREWS 5:7)

Choosing to submit to the authorities God has set up is a sign of great strength of character. Rebelling against God and the authorities he has set up is sin. It's a serious matter because it gives Satan an opportunity to attack. It is therefore in our own interests, for our own spiritual protection, that we make the choice to live under the authority of God and those he has placed over us.

Pride

When we were looking at forgiveness, I described as 'chilling' Jesus' words about handing over to the torturers those who refused to forgive. Here is a chilling verse from the Old Testament: 'Though the Lord is on high, he looks upon the lowly, but the proud he knows from afar' (Psalm 138:6). God keeps his distance from the proud. If we are proud we will not hear his voice, we will not know his closeness.

Pride is basically about thinking we can manage our own affairs without help from God or anyone else. If that is our attitude, God lets us get on with it. He knows that sooner or later we will discover the truth.

Trust in the Lord with all your heart, and do not lean on your own understanding. In all your ways acknowledge him, and he will make your paths straight. Do not be wise in your own eyes; fear the Lord and turn away from evil. (PROVERBS 3:5–7)

When we recognize the truth of how things are, we will know that we cannot accomplish anything of value on our own.

We will turn to God in complete dependence. We will live in humility. We may have the impression that humility means being a doormat, allowing others to walk all over us. That is not a good definition. Paul said, 'we put no confidence in the flesh' (Philippians 3:3) and that is a much better definition. We put no confidence in ourselves but choose instead to be 'strong in the Lord, and in the strength of his might' (Ephesians 6:10). Being humble does not mean being a doormat. It means putting our confidence in God, where it belongs.

Pride is the original sin of the devil. It sets one person or group against another – prejudice and bigotry are forms of pride. We hate to admit that there may be prejudice or bigotry in our hearts, but it's another area where we need to come clean and be honest with God so that Satan does not gain any advantage in our lives.

Sin–confess cycles

Our relationship to sin
We now come to look at a big issue for many of us, the whole question of dying to sin and getting rid of those depressing cycles where we sin, confess it, then sin again...and again... and end up feeling hopeless and miserable.

First of all, let's understand our relationship to sin as Christians. Let's go through some verses in Romans 6, a key passage to understand:

> If we have been united with him like this in his death, we will certainly also be united with him in his resurrection. For we know that our old self was crucified with him so that the body of sin might be done away with, that we should no longer be slaves to sin – because anyone who has died has been freed from sin. (ROMANS 6:5–7)

We have been united with Christ both in his death and in his resurrection, his new life. Have you died with Christ? Yes? Good! Then according to that passage, you have also been freed from sin. 'Well, I don't feel very free.' It is not about feelings. It's about truth – read the last sentence of that passage again. If you have died with Christ, you have been (past tense!) freed from sin. Our old self was crucified with him. Deep down inside we have become someone new.

When slavery was abolished, there were technically no slaves from that day on. They were all free. But how many of them continued to live like slaves? Most of them. Because it wasn't easy to start a different way of life. And they still felt like slaves.

It's like that with us too. Our old self died. We have been set free from sin. If you make a commitment to believe that truth, it will work out in your experience. The starting point, as always, is what God says is true:

> *Now if we died with Christ, we believe that we will also live with him. For we know that since Christ was raised from the dead, he cannot die again; death no longer has mastery over him. The death he died, he died to sin once for all; but the life he lives, he lives to God.*   (ROMANS 6:8–10)

The fact that Jesus was resurrected proves that death has no mastery over him. When he went to the cross, he took all the sins of the world upon him. When he came back to life, there were no sins on him. As he sits at the right hand of the Father, there are no sins on him. 'He died to sin once for all.' He triumphed over both death and sin.

'If we died with Christ, we believe that we will also live with him.' The point of Paul's argument here is this: Jesus' resurrection demonstrated beyond all doubt complete victory over both death and sin; you died with him; you were also resurrected with him. Therefore you too have triumphed over both death and sin:

> *In the same way, count yourselves dead to sin but alive to God in*
> *Christ Jesus.*   (ROMANS 6:11)

We can count ourselves dead to sin because we have died with Christ and been raised to life with him. 'God made him who had no sin to be sin for us, so that in him we might become the righteousness of God' (2 Corinthians 5:21). Now we are just like him. Death has no mastery over us and neither does sin.

It's not the 'counting' ourselves dead to sin that makes us dead to sin. We count ourselves dead to sin because we are! The word 'count' here in the original text carries the meaning of 'go on continually counting'. We must continually believe the truth. When sin makes its appeal you can legitimately say, 'I don't have to do that.'

How can you die to sin? Well, actually you can't. Why not? You already have! A lot of Christians put huge effort into trying to be something they already are – dead to sin and alive to God. We spend our lives trying to do what Jesus has already done.

Watchman Nee, one of the greatest Christian writers, struggled for nine years to 'count himself dead to sin'. Finally, he got to the point where he said, 'I can't go on unless I really understand this. I'm going to get out of the ministry and give up preaching if I don't understand this.' Finally, one day he suddenly got it. He saw that dying to sin wasn't something that he still had to do or make happen. It was something that had already been done, it was a fact, and all he had to do was catch up with the reality of the situation. He said, 'Praise the Lord that I am dead!'

Martin Luther put it this way: 'We don't do anything. We don't give anything to God, but we receive and allow someone else to do all the work for us and in us and it's God that does it.'

Sin has not died – it still appeals to us in the form of the world, the flesh and the devil. But we have died to sin. When sin makes its appeal, we have power to say 'no'. Our relationship with sin ended when the Lord 'rescued us from the dominion of darkness and brought us into the kingdom of the Son he loves' (Colossians 1:13).

Up to now, Paul has given us nothing to do apart from believe the truth that he is telling us. Now he comes to something to do. In fact, he gives us two things not to do followed by two things to do:

> *Therefore do not let sin reign in your mortal body so that you obey its evil desires. Do not offer the parts of your body to sin, as instruments of wickedness, but rather offer yourselves to God, as those who have been brought from death to life; and offer the parts of your body to him as instruments of righteousness. For sin shall not be your master, because you are not under law, but under grace.*
> (ROMANS 6:12–14)

Although we are dead to sin, clearly we can still allow sin to reign in our bodies and we can choose to offer parts of our bodies to sin as instruments of wickedness. We don't have to, but we can.

The responsibility not to let sin reign is ours. God will not do it for us – he has already done everything he needs to do. We don't have a 'devil-made-me do-it' attitude – the responsibility is ours.

The question is, how do we not let sin reign? We are not to use our bodies in ways that would serve sin as 'instruments of unrighteousness'. If we do, we allow sin to reign in our physical bodies. We are, however, firstly to offer ourselves to God, and secondly to offer our bodies to him. We are told consciously to present ourselves to God, because we belong to him. Then we are to present our bodies to God. This whole concept of 'offering our bodies' either to sin or to God is like an offering at the altar. Paul talks about our being 'living sacrifices' (Romans 12:1).

Why does Paul separate 'ourselves' from our bodies? If we

swallow the Western worldview, we see ourselves as little more than our physical bodies, so we consider them one and the same. If we are not careful, when we become Christians, we do not change our thinking and still see ourselves as fundamentally consisting of just our physical body with a spiritual side added on. Consequently, we tend still to get our identity, our worth, our value and our acceptance from our physical being and what we do. However, that is not who we are. At the most fundamental level possible we, like God, are spirit. Our spirit will go on forever. Our physical body will not. We are spiritual beings who live in a physical body. There's a big difference.

Sexual sin

So we are not to use our bodies as 'instruments of unrighteousness'. Let's look at the whole area of sexual sin. It's difficult to think how you could commit a sexual sin without using your body as an instrument of unrighteousness. When we do that, we allow sin to reign in our body.

> The body is not meant for sexual immorality, but for the Lord, and the Lord for the body. By his power God raised the Lord from the dead, and he will raise us also. Do you not know that your bodies are members of Christ himself? Shall I then take the members of Christ and unite them with a prostitute? Never! Do you not know that he who unites himself with a prostitute is one with her in body? For it is said, 'The two will become one flesh.' But he who unites himself with the Lord is one with him in spirit.
>
> Flee from sexual immorality. All other sins a man commits are outside his body, but he who sins sexually sins against his own body. Do you not know that your body is a temple of the Holy Spirit, who is in you, whom you have received from God? You are not your own; you were bought at a price. Therefore honour God with your body. (1 CORINTHIANS 6:13–20)

We have more than just a spiritual union with God. Although we have said that they are temporary, our physical bodies are spiritually significant too. In fact, our bodies are 'members of Christ himself' and 'a temple of the Holy Spirit'. Sexual sin defiles God's temple.

What happens when a child of God (united with the Lord and one spirit with him) also unites with a prostitute and becomes one with her in body? They become 'one flesh' – they are bonded together. This bonding mechanism is a gift from God created specifically for a marriage relationship whereby a man and a woman commit themselves to each other before him. Using it outside that relationship, either with a prostitute as in Paul's example or with anyone else, has consequences – a spiritual bonding takes place.

What does that mean in practice? As you would expect, like any other sin, sexual sin gives the enemy a foothold that he can use to gain influence in our minds. However, it seems to do more than that. It can serve to draw us back to the same person or to the same sin again and again.

How many times have you come across someone who is clearly unhappy in a sexual relationship outside marriage and wants to break it off but somehow never can, or, even if they do, end up going back to a partner who they know is going to mistreat them in some way? They are bonded, they are one flesh. There would still be a hold and a pull back even if they did manage to break the relationship.

We can, however, take back ground that we have given to the enemy. Even when we have defiled God's temple, in his grace he can make us completely pure again. We need to close the doors we have opened to the enemy and break any sinful bonds that we have formed. We can then present our bodies back to God as living sacrifices, committing, as far as sexual activity is concerned, to reserve them exclusively for marriage.

If you are not married, keep your body as a gift for your

future spouse, should God provide one for you. You are too special to allow it to be defiled.

The wonderful thing is that no matter how many past sexual experiences you may have had or what they were, Christ resolves them completely. You are no longer dirty or unacceptable.

Breaking sin–confess cycles

What happens if we do allow sin to reign in our body? We get a sin–confess cycle. Paul describes what this feels like in Romans 7. Many have argued that Paul is describing his experience before he was a Christian in this passage, but simply look at verse 22: 'in my inner being I delight in God's law.' I can't think of a non-Christian who would say that. I think Paul is simply being honest about the predicament that all Christians know, the sin–confess cycle.

> *I do not understand what I do. For what I want to do I do not do, but what I hate I do. And if I do what I do not want to do, I agree that the law is good.* (ROMANS 7:15–16)

You would be hard pressed to find a better description than that of what it feels like to be in bondage to sin. Here is someone who knows what is right and wants to do what is right but for some reason just can't.

> *As it is, it is no longer I myself who do it, but it is sin living in me. I know that nothing good lives in me, that is, in my flesh.* (ROMANS 7:17)

Paul is going out of his way here to show that what you might call 'the real him' – the new creation in Christ – is not the one causing this predicament. This new creation, who he really is, is not the one that has 'nothing good' living in him. He has plenty of good things living in him – God's Holy Spirit, for a start! It is his flesh that has nothing good in it. This is important. If we see ourselves as no good or in some way compelled to sin, we will just give up and believe that it is hopeless. His flesh is not part of 'the real him'. It's a residue from his old life. It's the old set of thought patterns that he developed when he was living independently of God, trying to meet his legitimate needs for significance, security and acceptance through things other than God. When he dies, he will no longer have the flesh. He does not have to give in to the flesh any longer, but if he allows it to reign in his body, this is the result:

> *For I have the desire to do what is good, but I cannot carry it out. For what I do is not the good I want to do; no, the evil I do not want to do – this I keep on doing. Now if I do what I do not want to do, it is no longer I who do it, but it is sin living in me that does it.*
> (ROMANS 7:18B–20)

Whose responsibility is it not to allow sin to reign in his body in the first place? It is his. But if he does allow sin to reign, he gets into this awful predicament where he appears not to be in control of his actions:

> *So I find this law at work: When I want to do good, evil is right there with me.* (ROMANS 7:21)

Is he saying that he is evil? No, he is saying there is evil present with him. Satan is always ready to tempt us into sin. The flesh is forever pulling us towards sin. The world wants to entice us into sin. Those things are always present, always looking for an opportunity. When we want to do good, up they pop. They do it so consistently that Paul calls it a 'law':

> *For in my inner being I delight in God's law.* (ROMANS 7:22)

One of the hallmarks of the new covenant that God has made through Jesus Christ is that his Law is now written on our hearts rather than on tablets of stone. Because the Holy Spirit lives in us and is united with our spirit, we really want to do what is right. When we do things that are contrary to our new nature – when we act out of character, as it were – the Holy Spirit immediately brings conviction because of our union with God. Note that he never brings condemnation. Just a gentle conviction of what is right.

> ... but I see another law at work in the members of my body, waging war against the law of my mind and making me a prisoner of the law of sin at work within my members.
>
> (ROMANS 7:23)

The problem here is that we have allowed sin to reign in our bodies. The enemy has a foothold. So a kind of law takes effect: whenever we rejoice in doing right in our inner person, our body reacts against that and instead wants to lead us into more sin. Notice how it does this – it wages war against the (good) law of my mind. This is a battle for the mind.

> What a wretched man I am! Who will rescue me from this body of death? Thanks be to God – through Jesus Christ our Lord! So then, I myself in my mind am a slave to God's law, but in the flesh a slave to the law of sin.
>
> (ROMANS 7:24–25)

A sin–confess cycle is an utterly miserable predicament. Despite the good intentions in your inner person, 'the real you', you have given your body over to sin and the flesh has taken over and there is a huge conflict. It doesn't have to be like that.

The way out

Is there a way out? Absolutely! As Paul says, 'Who will rescue me from this body of death? Thanks be to God – through Jesus Christ our Lord!' And he continues:

Therefore, there is now no condemnation for those who are in Christ Jesus, because through Christ Jesus the law of the Spirit of life set me free from the law of sin and death.

(ROMANS 8:1–2)

It is not as if what Paul calls 'the law of sin and of death' which pulls us towards sin has gone away. But we have access to a greater law, a more powerful law, 'the law of the Spirit of life in Christ Jesus'. Normally we cannot fly because the law of gravity prevents us. However, when we get into a plane, we find we can fly. The law of gravity has not been suspended but we overcome it by a greater law, that of aerodynamics and the forward thrust of the engine. Although the law of sin and death is still working, we have access to a greater law and can fly above sin and death by the power of the Spirit of life.

Although it feels as if there is nothing we can do to get out of the predicament, the truth is that we do not have to let the flesh rule. If we have allowed sin to reign in our bodies, we can put a stop to it.

The starting point as always is to know the truth. The truth is that we are dead to sin. Our relationship with sin has ended, and if we are caught in sin we are acting out of character.

Confess and resist

When we get stuck in one of these cycles and we sin yet again, the first thing we generally do is say sorry to God. We have confessed what we have done. Then we ask God to forgive us. He forgives us. In fact, we were already forgiven. If that is all we do, then we will probably fall for the sin again.

Imagine that you come across a door that says, 'Danger. Do not open.' You are intrigued. You really want to know what is on the other side of the door. You know you shouldn't but eventually temptation gets the better of you and you open the door. Immediately, a monster with a big mouth full of teeth escapes from behind the door and fastens itself onto your arm. It hurts.

When you give into temptation and sin, you open the door to the enemy. You give him a foothold. He fastens onto you and does not let go.

Our Western worldview has conditioned us not to see the involvement of the enemy. When we fall for a sin, we tend to overlook the fact that we have now given him a foothold in our mind, that he has fastened himself onto us with his big teeth. What do we do? We confess, 'I'm sorry I did that, Lord. Would you forgive me?' God says, 'Of course.'

You have confessed and agreed with God that you opened the door. You have received forgiveness. But the monster is still fastened to your arm and the door is still open. All you have done so far is to submit to God. However, James 4:7 says, 'Submit to God. Resist the devil, and he will flee from you.' There is more to be done!

Repentance isn't complete until you've done more than simply confess, which is just agreeing with God that you did it. You also need to resist the devil, causing him to flee from you so that his influence is removed. As you go through The Steps and repent of past sin, then tell the enemy to leave your presence, you will do just that. For many this is the first time they have been beyond simply confessing.

Do not condemn yourself

Continuing the analogy above, if a monster fastened itself onto your arm, you'd probably start hitting it, trying to get it to release its grip and go. What, however, if the monster was invisible and all you knew was that you had opened the door and now you were in a lot of pain and could not function normally? Whom would you hit out at now? Yourself, probably: 'You idiot. Why didn't you obey the sign? You're such a loser!' Or possibly God: 'You could have stopped me making that mistake – why didn't you? You could stop this pain and you aren't!'

If you think that you are the only one involved in the problem, you will lash out at yourself or God. You will look for the solution only in yourself or God. We need, however, to take all of reality into account. There is more going on. It is not just you and God who are involved.

Rather than attacking the monster, because we don't recognize that it is there, we tend to turn on ourselves. 'You pathetic individual, aren't you ever going to get over this?' People eventually get tired of beating themselves up, so they walk away from God under a cloud of defeat and condemnation.

Much of the time we believe (wrongly) that God's patience is exhausted, that he has given up on us. His patience with us is never exhausted. He never gives up on us.

This is the truth: 'there is now no condemnation for those who are in Christ Jesus' (Romans 8:1). God does not condemn us for our mistake. Not even a bit. He simply dusts us down, gives us a reassuring hug and helps us on our way.

It is not as if our sin did not matter. It did. It had serious consequences for us and our fruitfulness. But it did not change our relationship with God.

God's acceptance of you in no way depends on your behaviour.

Continue to resist
We then need to continue to resist the devil and temptation. The sins that typically lead to these sin–confess cycles come as a result of our trying to meet our needs independently of God. We have not believed that Christ can meet all our needs. Instead of pursuing and cultivating a relationship with Christ, we have chosen to try to find comfort or feel better independently of him. Part of our ongoing resistance is to renew our minds so that we continually commit ourselves to the truth that Christ does meet all our needs.

Where sin has been a habit, it remains an ongoing vulnerability. We become less vulnerable over time, but in the early days especially it can be very helpful to make ourselves accountable to a trusted fellow-Christian. Just knowing that you will get a call once a week saying, 'How have you done in that area?' gives us an extra impetus to commit ourselves to the truth.

There may be other practical measures we need to take too. For those who have been stuck in internet porn, consider making someone else responsible for the security level on your computer so that you cannot any longer access those kinds of sites.

Be filled with the Spirit

As we move forward, we remain vulnerable to falling back into the same old sins. It is helpful to remind ourselves that we do not have to, and of the key principle when it comes to the flesh: 'Live by the Spirit, and you will not gratify the desires of the flesh' (Galatians 5:16).

We are tempted to return to a law concept. If we have been giving in to lustful thoughts, we tend to say, 'I must not give in to lustful thoughts.' In fact, all we are doing is creating a law. The liberating New Testament concept is not to make a law but instead to choose to be filled with the Spirit: 'Where the Spirit of the Lord is, there is freedom' (2 Corinthians 3:17).

As we walk away from sin–confess cycles, it is helpful to keep presenting our bodies as living sacrifices to God, reminding ourselves that our bodies are temples of the Holy Spirit and asking the Holy Spirit to keep filling us.

Addiction

Addictions are particularly deep-rooted sin–confess cycles. Like other strongholds, they usually start as coping mechanisms. Very often they are used to cope with emotional pain.

As with any other sin, however, we can expect to see them completely resolved in Christ.

Sometimes it is enough for an addict to understand who they are in Christ. Once you realize that you are simply a product of Christ's work on the cross and not a product of the past, much of the pain of past experiences is taken away. Usually, however, it is necessary to do more work, but the approach is the same as for other sin–confess cycles.

I have seen Christians kick addictions to binge-eating, anorexia, drugs, alcohol and other things through understanding their identity in Christ, then submitting to God and resisting the devil. I have every admiration for Alcoholics Anonymous and the great work they do. However, I have come to realize that if it's a Christian who has the alcohol issue, although they very much do need to own up to the problem, it is not necessarily helpful for them to identify themselves as 'an alcoholic' as if that were part of their identity. The truth is that they are not an alcoholic – their fundamental identity is that of a child of God. A correct assessment would be to say that they are a child of God with an alcohol problem. That problem can be fully resolved in Christ. They do not have to drink. Instead they can be filled with the Spirit. The alcohol problem is not part of who they are. In fact it goes right against who they are – in drinking to excess they are acting completely out of character.

Here is the story of a Christian who had been struggling with smoking:

> I had had numerous failed attempts at stopping smoking since I'd restarted again but I couldn't even last 24 hours. I was extremely embarrassed that I smoked, especially as I was leading so many Freedom Appointments and yet wasn't walking in complete freedom myself.
>
> Anyway, last May I sat down with God. I had sussed out that when I thought about certain people or events, or anything sometimes, I would get what felt like a physical

sensation inside which was extremely unpleasant, a bit like dread and fear and loss, and which smoking got rid of instantly.

I've been taught well by Freedom In Christ and know that what I'm thinking about will have a direct impact on my feelings so I knew it was to do with my thoughts and the battle for my mind. So I asked God about His advice to take every thought captive in obedience to Jesus. The way I'm wired, to be able to do something I need to be able to understand what He means. So I asked Him what He meant.

He said, 'If you were in the army and you caught an enemy, you wouldn't take him back to your quarters and sit him in the corner of your room and have a chat with him. No, what you'd do, without hesitation, would be to take that enemy to the place your Commanding Officer had designated for him. Well, you're in My army and your Commanding Officer is Jesus, so all that is required of you is for you to obediently take every captured thought to Jesus and he'll deal with them.' And it was that simple. I soon became very aware of what was going on in my mind whereas before I let it wander around all over the place. I put a kind of mental butterfly net in there and could almost see myself catching thoughts and then I'd say something like 'Jesus, I've caught these thoughts and I'm giving them to you obediently' and within seconds the feelings that had risen up in me were replaced with peace and hence the desire to grab a cigarette was gone. Often when the battle was really intense, I didn't feel like I was doing much else than catch thoughts but I did my part, God did the miracle bit. I've no idea how he did the miracle bit, but, together we did it, and I've not smoked for over 13 months. Praise Him.

Inherited consequences of sin

The Bible is clear that the consequences of sin (not the guilt for them) pass down generations. In other words, we can inherit vulnerability to a particular sin from our parents and more distant ancestors in much the same way that we have all inherited the consequences of Adam's sin.

This is another area which the Western worldview predisposes us to overlook because it is not within our experience. The result is that it is all too easy to leave these spiritual vulnerabilities in place when they could be dealt with straightforwardly.

None of us has any difficulty recognizing that we have a genetic inheritance from our ancestors. Our genes determine our physical characteristics and, according to scientists, can determine our vulnerability to certain character traits. It is claimed, for example, that certain gene combinations make it more likely that someone will become an alcoholic. However, nobody claims that they make this inevitable. Personal choice is ultimately more important than the genes.

We also recognize that the environment we were brought up in has a significant effect on our character and values. As Jesus said, 'A student is not above his teacher, but everyone who is fully trained will be like his teacher' (Luke 6:40). That too is something that we inherit from past generations and something that we can choose to perpetuate or not.

As in many areas of life, the same principles that apply in the physical realm apply in the spiritual realm too. There are many places in the Old Testament that explicitly outline the principle of the consequences of sin passing down generations, the most significant being in the Ten Commandments themselves:

You shall not make for yourself an idol in the form of anything in heaven above or on the earth beneath or in the waters below. You

shall not bow down to them or worship them; for I, the Lord your
God, am a jealous God, punishing the children for the sin of the
fathers to the third and fourth generation of those who hate me,
but showing love to a thousand generations of those who love me
and keep my commandments.

(EXODUS 20:4–6 [SEE ALSO EXODUS 34:6–7])

God blesses obedience to a thousand generations but, in his grace, allows the effects of sin to pass down only three or four generations. Yet it is clear that they do pass down.

Jeremiah also makes clear that God brings 'the punishment for the fathers' sins into the laps of their children after them' (Jeremiah 32:17–18). What exactly is happening here? Are we talking genetics, environment or some other effect? The word used here translated as 'laps' has historically been translated 'bosom'. It has the sense of being 'inside' – the inner person, if you like. Elsewhere it is translated 'heart' (e.g. Isaiah 40:11). The implication is that this effect is neither genetic nor environmental but spiritual. Another passage makes this even clearer:

You will perish among the nations; the land of your enemies will
devour you. Those of you who are left will waste away in the
lands of their enemies because of their sins; also because of their
fathers' sins they will waste away.

But if they will confess their sins and the sins of their fathers
– their treachery against me and their hostility toward me, which
made me hostile toward them so that I sent them into the land of
their enemies – then when their uncircumcised hearts are humbled
and they pay for their sin, I will remember my covenant with Jacob
and my covenant with Isaac and my covenant with Abraham, and
I will remember the land.

(LEVITICUS 26:38–42)

Confession of their own sins and the sins of their ancestors leads to an annulment of the negative effects that have been handed down to them. In other words, we are dealing here with a spiritual issue.

Hosea takes this further and seems to imply that the sin of an ancestor leads directly to a predisposition to that kind of sin in their descendants:

> They consult a wooden idol and are answered by a stick of wood. A spirit of prostitution leads them astray; they are unfaithful to their God. They sacrifice on the mountaintops and burn offerings on the hills, under oak, poplar and terebinth, where the shade is pleasant. Therefore your daughters turn to prostitution and your daughters-in-law to adultery.
>
> (HOSEA 4:12–13)

Note the 'therefore' in the last sentence. The cause of the daughters' sexual sin is 'a spirit of prostitution' that is a direct result of the parents' idolatry (i.e. spiritual prostitution).

However, wherever you find the effect of sin being passed down generations, it is always clear that by turning away from the sin, the effects are cancelled out. Godly people frequently confessed their own sins, the sins of their ancestors and the sins of the nation.

In the time of Ezekiel, the people had become fatalistic and refused to take responsibility for their own lives. They understood the principle of the effects of sin coming down the generations but had taken it too far. They quoted a (non-biblical) proverb to justify their own sin:

> The word of the Lord came to me: 'What do you people mean by quoting this proverb about the land of Israel: "The fathers eat sour grapes, and the children's teeth are set on edge"? As surely as I live, declares the Sovereign Lord, you will no longer quote this proverb in Israel. For every living soul belongs to me, the father as well as the son – both alike belong to me. The soul who sins is the one who will die.' (EZEKIEL 18:1–4)

The proverb implied that they had no choice but to sin and that was that. They were saying in effect that their own sins were not their own fault but were due to the sins of their ancestors. Ezekiel is clear that this is not true. Despite the effects of our ancestors' sins, one principle shines through the Old Testament, and that is that each person is responsible for their own life and therefore their own sin. We are not guilty for the sins of our forefathers and we don't inevitably have to follow suit. We have a choice.

In the New Testament we find instances of people having been affected by evil spirits from a very young age (Mark 7:24–30; 9:14–29; Matthew 17:14–18). Given that a demon cannot have influence where it has not been given grounds, what could the cause of this influence be in ones so young? We are not told, but an issue coming down from previous generations seems likely. There is an interesting exchange in John 9:1–3:

> *As he went along, he saw a man blind from birth. His disciples asked him, 'Rabbi, who sinned, this man or his parents, that he was born blind?'*
>
> *'Neither this man nor his parents sinned,' said Jesus, 'but this happened so that the work of God might be displayed in his life.'*

The disciples ask Jesus whether it was the parents' sin or the man's sin that caused him to be born blind, reflecting the standard belief of the day that the effects of sin passed down the generations (see also Matthew 27:24–25 for a further indication of that belief in the crowd calling for Jesus to be crucified). Jesus corrects them – but crucially, not for holding the belief itself. He does, however, tell them that they are taking it too far – not every illness can be blamed on the effect of ancestral sin. In this case, the man was born blind so that God's glory might be revealed.

Paul explains that positive spiritual blessings pass down from Christian parents to children (1 Corinthians 7:14–15).

This is an example of the same principle operating, but with a good spiritual heritage rather than a bad one.

But, some may say, didn't Jesus deal with our sin at the cross? Yes. He dealt with our guilt. But we never were guilty for the sins of our ancestors – each person is responsible for their own sin. But that sin may cause consequences for others in much the same way that someone who was physically harmed by a mugger may walk with a limp – they were not guilty for that sin but they suffer the consequences.

Each one of us, then, is born with genetic, environmental and spiritual dispositions. These can be good or bad. We need actively to take a stand against the bad elements of our inheritance – otherwise we simply leave them in place and they remain effective. In particular, we need to take steps to deal with any footholds of the enemy that we inherited as a result of past sin, in order to make sure the enemy cannot hold us back.

Given that in Christ we have much more spiritual power and authority than the enemy does, this is not a difficult issue. We simply ask the Holy Spirit to make us aware of what the issues are and then actively renounce them.

It is simple and straightforward, but for some people it makes an enormous difference. A good friend of mine began experiencing headaches and severe spiritual 'interference' during the Steps To Freedom process. He sensed that the Holy Spirit was saying that there was Freemasonry (which is steeped in the occult) in his family background. As soon as he renounced it, the interference and headaches stopped.

I can think too of a Christian couple who had some issues in their marriage. He had already been married twice before and, as he looked back at his family line, he realized that on both sides of his family as far back down the generations as he could remember, there was divorce. As he came to renounce divorce, he experienced real spiritual opposition and struggled even to say the word. However, as soon as he had, the opposition disappeared. He realized that he had entered his present marriage with something of a caveat – 'Well, if it doesn't work, we can always get divorced.' Afterwards, he and his wife renewed their wedding vows and have gone on to maintain a firm emphasis on 'till death us do part' in their now strong marriage.

This is one area that most of us simply have never had any teaching on. The result is that we leave the enemy some ability to hold us back when we simply don't have to.

In this section we have looked at the areas in our life where the enemy may be able to hold us back. Remember, the effects of that will be in our mind and, because he is the master of deception, we probably do not even recognize them. It is only when we humbly come to God and ask him to reveal to us what the problems are, that many of them become apparent for the first time. The good news is that the Steps To Freedom In Christ process is a kind, gentle and usually matter-of-fact one that helps us to exercise the amazing spiritual authority we now have and to deal with those problems.

There is nothing too big for you and God!

Renew Your Mind

A comprehensive process of repentance such as The Steps To Freedom is just a starting point. The principles are ones we should all be taught as soon as we become Christians so that we dump all the accumulated rubbish and take away the enemy's ability to hold us back, right at the start of our Christian life.

The biblical principles behind The Steps need to become a way of life. I try to go through the process once a year as a kind of spiritual check-up. We need to be able to deal with sin issues as they come up. If I am walking along and I suddenly remember something from the past involving someone I haven't forgiven, I simply do it there and then. If I fall for one of my fleshly vulnerabilities, I have learned there and then to submit to God through confessing and then to resist the enemy by renouncing the sin and commanding him to leave my presence.

The point of dumping the rubbish from the past is not so much that we feel better (though we do) but so that we can become fruitful, mature disciples of Jesus Christ and bring glory to him.

The difference between freedom and maturity

Any Christian can become an old Christian – you just have to wait long enough! Any Christian can become a mature Christian – but many do not. A pastor whose church is filled with mature Christians has a great asset. But one whose church is full of Christians who have simply got old without maturing has trouble on his hands! Babies are cute. But if they continue to behave like babies as they grow up, they become a lot less attractive.

Baby Christians need to be fed on spiritual milk but it should not be long before they are able to move on to meat. Paul and the writer to the Hebrews both expressed frustration that the people in churches they were responsible for were staying at the milk stage. That would be even more true in most of our churches today, I suspect.

How many pastors does it take to change a light bulb? Just one. But the light bulb has really got to want to change... (I'm sorry, I am working on my stronghold for telling truly awful jokes, but that one caught me unawares and just snuck in, and I can't bring myself to delete the poor little thing.)

Do you want to become mature? Actually, simply desperately wanting to change, wanting to become mature is not enough: no matter how much a young child might want to move on to solid food, if its stomach is still not able to receive it, the child may swallow the food but it will come straight back up undigested.

No matter how much you want to, it is impossible to become mature – to move on to the 'meat' – if you have not first taken hold of our freedom in Christ. If you go through a process such as The Steps To Freedom and honestly deal with the personal and spiritual conflicts that the Holy Spirit shows you, then you will be free and able to move on.

Being free, however, does not mean that you are mature. There is a great difference between freedom – which can be obtained in a relatively short time – and maturity, which is the work of a lifetime.

Maturity is a process of growth that continues throughout our lives as we apply ourselves to knowing God and his Word. A person might have been a Christian for four days or forty years, but they are still maturing.

Freedom, however, is a position we take in response to Christ's victory over sin and Satan. We are either free or bound in various areas of our lives. We don't grow into freedom in these areas: we take possession of freedom by the authority we have in Christ, wherever we realize that we have been deceived and bound.

Yet freedom and maturity are inextricably linked. If we do not first take hold of our freedom, we cannot mature.

Identifying lies

The first step in going on towards maturity is making sure we stand firm and do not give ground back to the enemy.

When I first met Rachel, she was the epitome of a Christian who had lost all hope. She was covered in bandages from injuries that she had inflicted on herself. She had difficulty stringing two sentences together because of drug abuse. She had suffered from eating disorders for years. In fact, it's a miracle she was alive at all.[1]

I was present when she went through The Steps To Freedom in the church that took her in and saw her through to her healing. I remember saying to her after her freedom appointment that she seemed to have believed the lie that she was dirty.

She surprised me with the vehemence of her response: 'No, that's not right at all!'

'Oh,' I said, 'it's just that you seem to have mentioned feeling dirty a lot.'

'Well,' she said, 'I *am* dirty. It's not a lie!'

Past experiences had taught Rachel to see herself and her body as dirty. Her subsequent anorexia, self-harm and addictions were simply ways she used to try to cope with – that is, blot out – those negative feelings.

By going through the Steps process she had kicked the

enemy out of her life and was now free, but if she had been left at that point, still believing the lie that she was dirty, what would have happened? She would almost certainly have spiralled back down into her former coping mechanisms, because the pain of feeling dirty would still have been there.

The key to her ongoing freedom was to know what is really true: that through Christ, she has been made pure, spotless and perfectly clean; that God welcomes her into his presence and is proud of her as his growing child.

For Rachel the lie was deeply ingrained. It was a real stronghold. She had taken the false assumption that she was dirty as fact for so long that she had to make an effort to start to believe what was really true. Yet, once she had closed the doors to the enemy's influence in her life, she was able to do that. Today, four years or so on, Rachel is doing well. She occasionally calls to keep in touch. When she does, I usually ask her, 'By the way, Rachel. Are you dirty?' She will always respond, 'No! I've been washed clean by the blood of the Lamb. Praise God!'

How are Christians transformed? Paul says clearly that it's through renewing their minds (Romans 12:2). It's as we commit ourselves wholeheartedly to believe what is true and throw out old ways of thinking, that we are changed to become more like Jesus. For Rachel, for me and for any Christian, that process of transformation takes time. We all have moments when we go backwards. But as long as we have learned that God does not condemn us and that we can pick ourselves up, dust ourselves down and carry on, we will all stay on that path of maturity.

The first step to renewing our minds and getting rid of the lies we have believed is identifying those lies. Rachel went through the whole appointment but it still had not dawned on her that she was believing a lie. She needed some help in pointing that out, and that is one of the reasons why we recommend that, where possible, people should do The Steps process with others in attendance to encourage and to pray.

In fact, if you take other people through The Steps and you have a good grasp of truth yourself, you can become adept at spotting lies. I tend to write them down and let the person have them at the end so that they can go away and start that process of renewing their mind.

Lies come out all through the process, but the forgiveness step is often the main place. As people forgive from the heart, they are encouraged to tell the Lord how what was done to them made them feel and to stay with it until they have put every remembered pain on the table. I listen particularly for what people say after 'which made me feel'. Practically always you will see the same words coming up time after time: 'inadequate', 'inferior', 'useless', 'dirty', 'helpless', 'hopeless', 'evil'. Of course, not everything they say at that point is necessarily a lie, but when a word comes up again and again it's usually a sign of a scheme that the enemy has used against them, a particular vulnerability that they have. In fact, often it becomes clear that the enemy seems to have engineered circumstance after circumstance in people's lives to get them to believe that lie.

What are the lies that you have come to believe? Usually they fall into three categories. There are lies about yourself – that is to say, about who you now are in Christ. We tend to believe that we are still more like our old selves and have not caught up with the truth of what happened when we became Christians and our old self died. Then there are lies about God's character. I'm always surprised at how people's view of God seems to be so influenced by their view of their earthly father. None of us had perfect earthly fathers and we all need to bring our understanding of God into line with what is actually true. Then there are lies about Satan, which usually amount to ascribing far more power to him than he actually has.

Stronghold-busting: a strategy for renewing our minds

These lies that have become deeply ingrained are strongholds. They have become our default way of thinking. They act like the ruts made by a Land Rover in a field. Eventually the ruts become so deep that the Land Rover will simply follow them like a train on a track. It takes effort to steer out of the ruts and dismantle the strongholds, but it is absolutely possible for a Christian to do that, no matter how deeply ingrained the lies may be.

> *The weapons we fight with are not the weapons of the world. On the contrary, they have divine power to demolish strongholds. We demolish arguments and every pretension that sets itself up against the knowledge of God, and we take captive every thought to make it obedient to Christ.*
>
> (2 CORINTHIANS 10:4–5)

Note the emphasis that Paul puts here on our responsibility: we are to fight, actively demolish arguments and pretensions that set themselves up against truth, and take captive every thought. Wielding the weapons that God gives us takes application and effort. No one else can do it for us, though others can stand with us and encourage us as we do it.

Psychologists tell us that it takes around six weeks to form or break a habit. Once you have dealt with any footholds of the enemy, a mental stronghold is simply a habitual way of thinking. Can you break a habit? Of course – but it takes some effort over a period of time.

The best way I know to renew your mind is to take the truth of the Word of God and work with it over a six-week period, actively renouncing what you used to believe and announcing what is actually true. It's a strategy I call 'stronghold-busting' and we looked at it briefly in the second book in this series.

First of all, you need to determine the lie you have been

believing (any way you are thinking that is not in line with what God says about you in the Bible). In doing this, ignore what you feel but commit yourself wholeheartedly to God's truth.

Then, find as many Bible verses as you can that state the truth and write them down. A good concordance (or a helpful pastor) will come in useful.

Write a prayer or declaration based on the formula:

- I renounce the lie that...
- I announce the truth that...

It is, incidentally, much more effective if you can develop and write the stronghold-buster yourself rather than having someone do it for you. By all means get some help to find the verses, but make sure that the thought process that goes into the prayer or declaration is yours.

Finally, read the Bible verses and say the prayer/declaration every day for forty days, all the time reminding yourself that God is truth and that if he has said it, it really is true for you. Don't worry if you miss a day or two (this is not a legalistic ritual) but do persevere until you have completed a total of forty days. In fact, you may wish to go on longer, and you will almost certainly want to come back and do it again at some point in the future.

Let me share with you a couple of examples of stronghold-busters that I have put together for my own use. I recognize in myself a vulnerability to the world's lie that real security comes from having money. Having recognized the lie, I set about finding the truth. These are some of the verses I found:

Then he said to them, 'Watch out! Be on your guard against all kinds of greed; a man's life does not consist in the abundance of his possessions.' (LUKE 12:15)

> *No-one can serve two masters. Either he will hate the one and love the other, or he will be devoted to the one and despise the other. You cannot serve both God and Money.* (MATTHEW 6:24)

> *For the love of money is a root of all kinds of evil. Some people, eager for money, have wandered from the faith and pierced themselves with many griefs.* (1 TIMOTHY 6:10)

> *Keep your lives free from the love of money and be content with what you have, because God has said, 'Never will I leave you; never will I forsake you.'* (HEBREWS 13:5)

For those who are interested, I also listed Acts 4:32; Luke 12:20–21, 33–34; Philippians 4:12 and 1 John 3:17. Based on those verses, this is the prayer that I wrote:

> Lord, I recognize that the security that money offers is false and that the only lasting security is to be found in you. My life is not made meaningful by what I have but by the extent to which I honour you. I recognize that it is impossible to serve both God and Money – I choose to serve God with all my heart. I choose to be content with what I have – if very little, knowing that you provide my needs; if more than enough, ready to use it in your service. I choose to be rich towards you by honouring you with what you have entrusted to me. Thank you that you will never leave me or forsake me. Amen.

I prayed it through every day for forty days. I return to it from time to time when the issue crops up again.

A few years ago, a good Christian friend helped me understand that I had been operating in an arrogant way. I could not see it to start with, but then the Holy Spirit worked on me and it all became clear – horribly clear, to be honest! Here are some of the verses I found:

Pride goes before destruction, a haughty spirit before a fall. Better to be lowly in spirit and among the oppressed than to share plunder with the proud. (PROVERBS 16:18–19)

Pride only breeds quarrels, but wisdom is found in those who take advice. (PROVERBS 13:10)

For this is what the high and lofty One says – he who lives for ever, whose name is holy: 'I live in a high and holy place, but also with him who is contrite and lowly in spirit, to revive the spirit of the lowly and to revive the heart of the contrite.'

(ISAIAH 57:15)

Also in my list were: Proverbs 16:5; Proverbs 18:12; 2 Chronicles 7:14; Isaiah 66:2; Ephesians 4:2 and James 4:10. This is the prayer that I wrote:

Lord, I recognize that you detest the proud of heart, and that you live with those who have humble and contrite hearts. I now reject and renounce all the pride in me. I choose to humble myself under your mighty hand. I choose to take your yoke upon me. I choose to consider others as better than myself; to take advice from others; to bear with others in love. I now clothe myself in humility and humble myself under your mighty hand. I choose to pray and to seek your face, to turn from all sin. Cleanse me, O Lord, to the depths of my being from the sin of pride. Amen.

Remember that it takes time to demolish a stronghold and get rid of negative thinking. Just because the thoughts recur, doesn't mean it's not working – it's whether or not you choose to believe the thoughts that is important.

Ed Silvoso tells of how a pastor friend of his watched a concrete wall being demolished. It withstood ten, then fifteen, then thirty, then thirty-five blows with no visible sign of being weakened. That's how it can feel as you work through a strong-hold-buster day after day. However, each day you renounce the lie and commit yourself to truth is making a difference. A wall might appear not to have been weakened right up to, say, thirty-seven swings of a demolition ball. However, sooner or later (say on the thirty-eighth swing), a few small cracks will appear. On the next swing these cracks will get bigger until, finally, the wall completely collapses. Even though only the final three swings appear to have had an effect, without all the previous ones, the wall would not have fallen.

If you persevere with a stronghold-buster it will work – as long as you have first closed any doors open to the enemy, correctly identified the false belief and found genuine truth to replace it with. Don't treat this as some kind of magic, how-ever. It's not the speaking out that will change you, and there's not some special formula that works for everyone. Don't get all religious, either – if you miss a day or two, your righteous-ness has not been compromised. Just pick it up the next day and carry on. Don't get hung up on 'forty' as a magic number, either – do a stronghold-buster for at least forty days but carry on beyond that for as many days as it takes.

This strategy is effective only in so far as you seriously and methodically decide to reject lies and commit yourself to truth and persevere until you know that the stronghold has come down. But if you do that, you can dismantle every stronghold.

Taking a long-term view

One thing I love about this approach is that it works both for those who are carrying a lot of 'stuff' from the past and for those who do not have so much. From the pastor down to the most needy person in our church, we all need to commit ourselves to truth, resolve personal and spiritual conflicts and renew our minds. We can all expect to be fruitful and become the people God is calling us to be. No one is left out.

All of us, however, need to take a long-term view. Taking hold of your freedom in Christ is something that can happen relatively quickly. However, the processing of renewing your mind and maturing is something that you will spend the rest of your life doing.

> *Forgetting what is behind and straining towards what is ahead, I press on towards the goal to win the prize for which God has called me heavenwards in Christ Jesus. All of us who are mature should take such a view of things.*
>
> (PHILIPPIANS 3:13B–15A)

Paul often compared the Christian life to a race – not a sprint but a long-distance event, more of a marathon. We need to know where we are going – spiritual maturity – and, like Paul, commit ourselves to run the race for the long term.

We can now forget what has happened in the past. We are new creations. Once we resolve the personal and spiritual conflicts, we can stop dragging the past around with us. We are free to move on.

Let's 'strain towards what is ahead'. What is ahead? Becoming the person God is calling you to be – nothing and no one can get in your way because you already have everything you need to live the life he is calling you to (2 Peter 1:3; Ephesians 1:3). I look forward to the time when I will stand before Jesus at the end of my life or when he comes again. I hope to hear him say, 'Well done, good and faithful servant' (Matthew 25:21, 23).

In the next book in this series we will look at how we ensure that the goals we have for our life tie in with God's goals for us so that we become the people he is calling us to be, and how we relate to others as we work that out.

You may be thinking that you need to work on half a dozen stronghold-busters straight away. If you try to do that, you will burn out. Just like an athlete running a race, we need to pace ourselves. We can only start from where we are. It will take time to pull those strongholds down. But we don't have to do it all at once. Why not start with one that is the key issue for you and tear it down? Once you have done that, then do another one. Over the course of a year you could demolish seven or eight key lies that have up to now been default ways of behaving. Would that make a difference? You bet!

> *It is for freedom that Christ has set us free. Stand firm, then, and do not let yourselves be burdened again by a yoke of slavery.*
>
> (GALATIANS 5:1)

Go for it!

NOTE

1. Rachel's story is told in Eileen Mitson (ed.), *Songs of Freedom*, Monarch, 2004.

FREEDOM IN CHRIST *Discipleship Series*

Free to Be Yourself
ISBN: 978-1-85424-857-2

Win the Daily Battle
ISBN: 978-1-85424-858-9

Break Free, Stay Free
ISBN: 978-1-85424-859-6

The You God Planned
ISBN: 978-1-85424-860-2

These four short volumes can be read individually but also form a valuable accompaniment to the Freedom In Christ course.

Many Christians end up acting as they think a Christian should act – and finding that they simply can't keep it up. They either drop out or burn out. True fruitfulness comes from realizing that we became someone completely new the moment we became Christians. Living out the truth of who we now are makes all the difference.

The 'eternal life' that Jesus came to give us is not just something we get when we die. It's a whole different quality of life right now, a life which gives us perfect acceptance, phenomenal significance and complete security. Know the truth and choose to believe it and you can be the person you were made to be.

Available from your local Christian bookshop.

In case of difficulty, please visit the Lion Hudson website:
www.lionhudson.com/monarch

Freedom **Freedom In**
in Christ **Christ In The UK**

Church leaders – can we help you make disciples?

Although the Church may have made some *converts*, most will agree
that we have made few real *disciples*. Far too many Christians struggle
to take hold of basic biblical truth and *live it out*. It's not as if we lack
excellent teaching programmes. It's more to do with people's ability to
"connect" with truth. Or, as Jesus put it, "You will *know* the truth and
the truth will set you free." (John 8:32)

Many churches in the UK now use the Freedom In Christ approach to
help Christians make connections with truth and mature into fruitful
disciples. It works well as: a church-wide discipleship programme
using The Freedom In Christ Discipleship Course; a follow-up to
introductory courses like Alpha; a cell equipping track; or a small
group study.

If you are a UK church leader, we are at your disposal. We run a
regular programme of conferences and training, and are always happy
to offer advice.

Send for our catalogue

Send for our full colour catalogue of books, videos and audiocassettes.
It includes resources for churches and for individuals (including
children and young people and specialist areas such as depression
and addiction).

Join the Freedom Fellowship

For those using the Freedom In Christ approach, the Freedom
Fellowship provides advice on getting started in your church and
regular news and encouragement.

For details of any of the above, see www.ficm.org.uk, e-mail
info@ficm.org.uk or write to us at:
Freedom In Christ Ministries, PO Box 2842, READING RG2 9RT.

www.**ficm**.org.uk

*Freedom In Christ Ministries is a company limited by guarantee (number 3984116) and a registered
charity (number 1082555). It works by equipping local churches to help Christians claim their
freedom in Christ and become fruitful disciples.*